bake me I'm yours...
sweet bitesize bakes

Sarah Trivuncic

D&C
David and Charles
www.bakeme.com

Contents

bitten by the baking bug...

Since I became known as someone who bakes a lot, I've noticed how people's faces instantly light up when you talk about cakes. A shared love of making, admiring or enjoying cakes and cookies is a wonderful talking point. Most people have baked something before and many wish they were better, thinking that 'fancy stuff' is beyond their reach. I often encourage my friends that baking and cake decorating are accessible skills with great results for anyone prepared to practise a little.

Writing this book, I realized that while most people have baked sponges or biscuits, the majority will not have ventured far into cake decoration. The past three years – since I started writing my blog Maison Cupcake – has seen a huge surge in baking and cake decorating ranges available in high-street stores. I firmly believe that the only barrier to succeeding in your first sugarcraft projects is gathering the right equipment and taking a little time to experiment.

This book features a range of baking projects with simple decoration; even if you've never held a piping (pastry) bag or kneaded sugarpaste (rolled fondant) before you will find projects you can do in this book – they are graded with one to three spoons for how easy or difficult they are.

Once bitten by the baking and cake decorating bug, unless you have a big family or a community group to donate to, sharing treats out quicker than you can make them can be tricky. The beauty of small-scale bakes is that everyone can try a few things at once!

maisoncupcake.com

tools and equipment

Shown in this section is a selection of the baking and cake decorating equipment used in this book. Some items are needed for every project and others for a few specific ones; check the 'you will need' list for each project.

general baking equipment

1 Baking parchment

2 Sieve

3 Scales – preferably digital

4 Rolling pin

5 Electric mixer – large stand-alone model or handheld with a large bowl

6 Baking beans – for baking pastry cases 'blind'

7 Small palette knife – to lift cookies and spread buttercream

8 Wooden spoon and silicone spatula

9 Cocktail sticks (toothpicks)

10 Wire cooling rack

11 Baking sheets

12 20cm (8in) square cake tin (pan)

13 12-hole baking tins (pans) – sized accordingly

14 Madeleine or mini-madeleine tin (pan)

15 Cannelle mould

16 Metal cutters – circular and heart shaped in a variety of sizes

17 Paper cupcake cases

- Mini – for bitesize cakes – foil 20 x 32mm (¾ x 1¼in); paper 24 x 30mm (1 x 1⅛in)

- Standard – used for traditional fairy cakes – 25 x 45mm (1 x 1¾in)

- Muffin – used for larger American-style cupcakes – 45 x 49mm (1¾ x 2in)

18 Lollipop sticks – for cake pops

19 Polystrene or oasis block with holes – to stand cake pops in

- (Not pictured: double boiler for making chocolate ganache and marshmallow fluff and/ or plastic microwave saucepan for Candy Melts)

cake decorating equipment

1 Piping (pastry) bags – disposable, handmade paper or re-usable, with coupler

2 Piping tubes (tips) – selection of round, plus large star for piping buttercream swirls and roses or mini meringues, small star for piping mini pavlova nests

3 Miniature non-stick rolling pin – for rolling out sugarpaste

4 Square acrylic mat – to roll out small quantities of sugarpaste, also to cover cut-out pieces while working

5 A4 plastic sleeve cut at base so you can open like a book – for modelling sugarpaste petals

6 Pins – to pierce tubes (tips) if icing dries out

7 Plunger cutters – to cut out daisy and blossom shapes

8 Piping gun with syringe nozzle – for filling choux buns and fingers

9 Cocktail sticks (toothpicks) – to add food colouring to icing and sugarpaste

10 Zip-lock plastic bags and cling film (plastic wrap) – to wrap and store sugarpaste and stop it drying out

11 Sealable plastic tubs – for storing royal icing

12 Sticky labels – for identifying icing at a glance

13 Gel or paste food colourings

14 Lustre liquid, powder and sprays

15 Edible glitter

16 Cling film (plastic wrap)

17 Miscellaneous sugar baubles and sprinkles

18 Candy dipping tool

19 Crystallized rose and violet petals

20 Sugar thermometer – used for fondant icing

21 Chopstick – great for making tiny circles such as babies' eyes and nostrils

22 Fine brush – for applying lustre powders or liquids

23 Latex gloves – to prevent food colouring staining your hands

24 Plastic modelling tools – for shaping and modelling sugarpaste

bag it up...
You can buy re-usable piping (pastry) bags although many projects require several tiny bags so disposable paper ones are more practical.

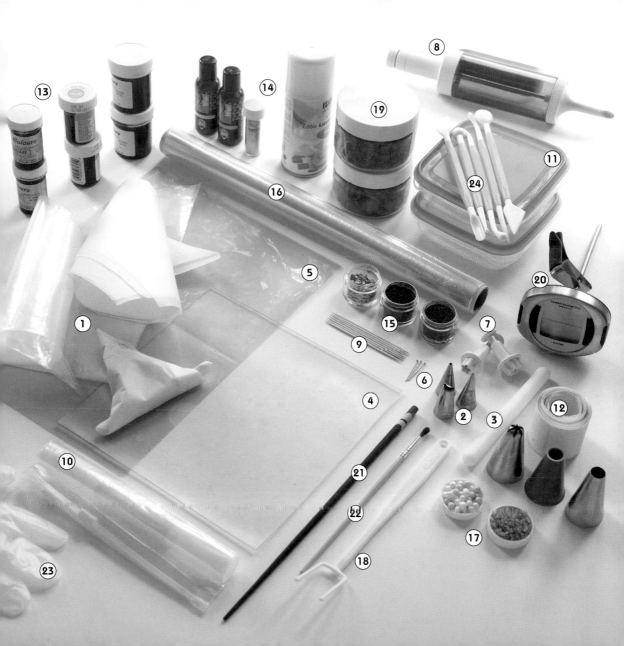

recipes

vanilla sponge cake

This classic vanilla sponge recipe forms the basis of many projects in this book; this recipe will yield 32 mini cupcakes, 18 standard cupcakes or 12 muffin-sized cupcakes. For a 20cm (8in) square cake for cutting into fondant fancies, increase the recipe quantities by 50 percent, using the table supplied. The sponge can be flavoured as desired (see flavour variations).

ingredients...	for cupcakes	for a 20cm (8in) square cake
unsalted (sweet) butter, softened	125g (4½oz)	180g (6½oz)
caster (superfine) sugar	125g (4½oz)	180g (6½oz)
large (US extra large) eggs, lightly beaten	2	3
vanilla extract	5ml (1 tsp)	7.5ml (1½ tsp)
self-raising (-rising) flour, sifted	125g (4½oz)	180g (6½oz)
milk	20ml (1½ tbsp)	30ml (2 tbsp)

1 Preheat the oven to 180°C/350°F/Gas 4. Take three 12-hole tins (pans) and line with 32 mini paper cupcake cases.

2 Using an electric mixer with a large bowl, cream the butter and sugar until pale and fluffy. Then beat in the eggs and vanilla extract.

play it cool...
Mini cupcakes are fragile when warm – allow them to cool completely before peeling away their cases.

3 Fold in the flour one-third at a time until just combined. Fold in the milk but do not over mix.

4 Evenly spoon the batter into the cases, filling them two-thirds full.

5 Bake in the oven for 12 minutes or until a cocktail stick (toothpick) inserted comes out clean.

6 Leave in the tins (pans) for a few minutes before transferring to a wire rack to cool completely.

fade to grey…
Some paper cases fade when baked so slip an extra one on after baking.

flavour variations

To change the flavour of your sponge, try the following alternatives:

- **Chocolate:** replace 25g (⅞oz) flour with 25g (⅞oz) cocoa powder (unsweetened cocoa) and replace the vanilla extract with chocolate extract.
- **Irish cream:** as for chocolate but replace the milk with Irish cream liqueur.
- **Lemon:** replace the vanilla extract with lemon extract and add the finely grated zest of one lemon to the flour.

baking times

If using this recipe to make larger cupcakes or a single cake, adjust the baking times to:

- 18 standard cupcakes – 16–18 minutes
- 12 muffin-sized cupcakes – 18–20 minutes
- 20cm (8in) square cake – 18–20 minutes

red velvet cake

As well as a traditional larger cake, vibrant red velvet sponge can be used for fondant fancies or cupcakes. Often paired with white marshmallow fluff (see Fillings and Toppings), this recipe makes 36 small sugarpaste-covered fondant fancies, 16 larger dipped fancies (with offcuts left over) or 25 red velvet hearts.

ingredients...

- ♡ 2.5ml (½ tsp) red paste food colouring
- ♡ 125ml (4fl oz) buttermilk
- ♡ 75g (2½oz) unsalted (sweet) butter, softened
- ♡ 150g (5¼oz) caster (superfine) sugar
- ♡ 2 medium eggs, separated
- ♡ 5ml (1 tsp) vanilla extract
- ♡ 125g (4½oz) plain (all-purpose) flour
- ♡ 15g (½oz) cornflour (cornstarch)
- ♡ 15ml (1 tbsp) cocoa powder (unsweetened cocoa)
- ♡ 2.5ml (½ tsp) baking powder
- ♡ pinch of salt
- ♡ 5ml (1 tsp) white wine vinegar
- ♡ 5ml (1 tsp) bicarbonate of soda (baking soda)

1 Preheat the oven to 180°C/350°F/Gas 4. Grease and line a 20cm (8in) square cake tin (pan) with baking parchment.

2 Mix the red paste food colouring and the buttermilk together. (Use paste food colouring to get a deep scarlet – liquid colouring cannot achieve this shade without spoiling the taste.)

3 Using an electric mixer with a large bowl, cream the butter and sugar until pale and fluffy. One by one, add the egg yolks and vanilla extract.

4 Sift the flour, cornflour (cornstarch), cocoa powder (unsweetened cocoa) and baking powder into a bowl.

5 Pulsing with the electric mixer, alternate between sifting in one-third of the dry ingredients and pouring in one-third of the buttermilk mix at a time until just fully incorporated.

red or dead...
Don't despair if the top appears brown after baking, a contrasting white icing on top will make the red colour stand out.

6 Whisk the egg whites and salt in a clean bowl until they form stiff peaks. Beat one-quarter of the egg white into the cake batter quickly to break some air then carefully fold in the remaining egg white one-quarter at a time using a metal spoon.

7 In a separate small bowl, mix the vinegar and bicarbonate of soda (baking soda) until bubbles form then swiftly but gently fold into the mix.

8 Pour evenly into the tin (pan) and pause for a minute to allow the bicarbonate of soda (baking soda) to work. Bake in the oven for 18–20 minutes or until a cocktail stick (toothpick) inserted comes out clean.

9 Leave the cake in the tin (pan) for a few minutes before turning out onto a wire rack to cool completely.

vanilla cookies

Cookies made from this dough are super easy to roll out and keep their shape in the oven. This recipe makes 45–65 cookies, depending on their size and shape, and can be flavoured as desired (see flavour variations).

ingredients...

- ♡ 175g (6oz) unsalted (sweet) butter, very soft
- ♡ 200g (7oz) caster (superfine) sugar
- ♡ 2 large (US extra large) eggs, beaten
- ♡ 5ml (1 tsp) vanilla extract
- ♡ 5ml (1 tsp) baking powder
- ♡ 5ml (1 tsp) salt
- ♡ 500g (1lb 1½oz) plain (all-purpose) flour plus extra for rolling out

1 Using an electric mixer with a large bowl, cream the butter and sugar until pale and fluffy then blend in the eggs and vanilla extract.

2 Stir the baking powder and salt into the flour and gradually mix into the batter to become dough.

3 Form the dough into two discs and chill for one hour wrapped in cling film (plastic wrap).

4 Towards the end of the chilling time, preheat the oven to 180°C/350°F/Gas 4. Grease and line several baking sheets with baking parchment.

5 Sprinkle a little extra flour on your work surface and rolling pin, and roll out each disc of chilled dough to an even 5mm (³⁄₁₆in) thickness. Cut into shapes as desired, placing them 3 4cm (1–1½in) apart on the baking sheets.

6 Bake for 8–10 minutes until lightly golden. Allow to cool on the sheet slightly before transferring to a wire rack to cool completely.

deep freeze...
If you don't need as many cookies, you can freeze half of the dough for up to two months.

flavour variations

To change the flavour of your cookies, try the following alternatives:

- **Chocolate:** replace 80g (2¾oz) flour with 80g (2¾oz) cocoa powder (unsweetened cocoa) and replace the vanilla extract with chocolate extract.
- **Orange and cardamom:** replace the vanilla extract with orange extract and add 2.5ml (½ tsp) ground cardamom to the flour.

easy does it...
If you use too much extra flour when rolling out, the dough will be less pliable – just a light dusting is all that's required.

gingerbread cookies

Beyond familiar gingerbread men, this dough is substantial enough to use for hanging cookies and even gingerbread houses. This recipe makes around 40 cookies, depending on their size and shape.

ingredients...

- ♡ 100g (3½oz) unsalted (sweet) butter
- ♡ 40g (1½oz) caster (superfine) sugar
- ♡ 40g (1½oz) soft (light) brown sugar
- ♡ 75g (2½oz) golden (corn) syrup or treacle (molasses), or half of each
- ♡ 200g (7oz) plain (all-purpose) flour plus extra for rolling out
- ♡ 3ml (⅔ tsp) bicarbonate of soda (baking soda)
- ♡ 5ml (1 tsp) ground ginger
- ♡ 2.5ml (½ tsp) ground cinnamon

1 Melt the butter, sugars, syrup and treacle (molasses) together in a medium-sized saucepan and set aside.

2 Sift the flour, bicarbonate of soda (baking soda) and spices in a large bowl. Pour in the melted butter and sugar mixture and stir into a dough.

3 Knead the dough, adding a few drops of water if required.

4 Form the dough into two discs and chill for 30 minutes wrapped in cling film (plastic wrap).

5 Halfway through the chilling time, preheat the oven to 180°C/350°F/Gas 4. Grease and line several baking sheets with baking parchment.

6 Sprinkle a little extra flour on your work surface and rolling pin, roll out each disc of chilled dough to an even 5mm (³⁄₁₆in) thickness. Cut into shapes as desired, placing them 3–4cm (1–1½in) apart on the baking sheets.

7 Bake for 10 minutes until golden. Allow to cool slightly before transferring to a wire rack to cool completely.

tough cookie...
This dough is prone to going hard in the fridge, so take care not to chill it for too long.

banana mini whoopie pie shells

These filled Amish cakes are traditionally chocolate with marshmallow filling, but you'll have everyone going bananas for this version. This recipe makes 24 filled mini whoopies (48 shells).

ingredients...

- ♡ 250g (8¾oz) plain (all-purpose) flour, sifted
- ♡ 2.5ml (½ tsp) bicarbonate of soda (baking soda)
- ♡ 2.5ml (½ tsp) baking powder
- ♡ 2.5ml (½ tsp) cinnamon
- ♡ pinch of salt
- ♡ 1 ripe banana
- ♡ 150ml (5fl oz) buttermilk
- ♡ 125g (4½oz) unsalted (sweet) butter, softened
- ♡ 100g (3½oz) caster (superfine) sugar
- ♡ 1 egg

1 In a large bowl, sift the flour, bicarbonate of soda (baking soda), baking powder, cinnamon and salt.

2 Using an electric hand blender, blitz the banana into the buttermilk until smooth.

3 Using an electric mixer with a large (separate) bowl, cream the butter and sugar until pale and fluffy. Beat the egg into the batter followed by the banana buttermilk mixture and mix until just smooth.

4 Stir in the dry ingredients until just combined and chill for at least 30 minutes.

5 Preheat the oven to 180°C/350°F/Gas 4. Grease and line several baking sheets with baking parchment or lightly grease mini whoopie pie tins (pans).

6 Using two teaspoons, drop heaped teaspoons of chilled batter onto the baking sheets or into the wells of the tins (pans) until you have 48 shells in total.

7 Bake the shells in the centre of the oven for 8–10 minutes until the cakes spring back to the touch. Allow to cool slightly before transferring to a wire rack to cool completely.

perfect pies...
Using a mini whoopie pie tin (pan) will give uniform results although you get flatter shells and a tasty crust without one.

mini meringues

Meringue is a simple mix of beaten egg white and sugar but a spotlessly clean bowl is essential for success. Metal bowls are less likely to retain smears of grease, and cream of tartar encourages the whites to build air. This recipe makes enough meringue for 24 nests or one big pavlova.

ingredients...

♡ 3 large (US extra large) egg whites

♡ 150g (5¼oz) caster (superfine) sugar

♡ large pinch of cream of tartar

1 Preheat the oven to 140°C/275°F/Gas 1. Grease and line two baking sheets with baking parchment.

2 Using an electric mixer and a spotlessly clean large bowl, beat the egg whites to a light foam before gradually adding the cream of tartar. Continue to whisk to a soft-peak meringue before adding 15ml (1 tbsp) sugar. Whisk again to a stiff peak meringue, finally folding in the remaining sugar with a metal spoon.

3 Fill a piping (pastry) bag fitted with a 1.5cm (½in) star tube (tip) with the meringue mixture and pipe 5cm (2in) nests 5cm (2in) apart on the baking sheets.

4 Place on a low shelf in the pre-heated oven and immediately reduce the heat to 120°C/250°F/Gas ½.

5 Bake for 20 minutes. The meringues should still be white, becoming more solid but still 'give' slightly when prodded. Turn the oven off and leave inside to cool completely.

tasty fillings...
Alternatively, pipe the meringue with a star tube (tip) in swirls and sandwich together in pairs with coloured buttercream or ganache (see Fillings and Toppings).

french macarons

These elegant Parisian almond meringues are sandwiched together in pairs with soft fillings – ganache, buttercream, crème patissière, jam, curd... anything! This recipe makes up to 48 shells (24 pairs), which can be flavoured to suit (see flavour variations).

ingredients...

- ♡ 110g (3¾oz) icing (confectioners') sugar, sifted
- ♡ 60g (2oz) ground almonds
- ♡ 2 egg whites (60g/2oz worth), ideally left to age for 24 hours loosely covered in a cool place or several days in the fridge but brought back up to room temperature before use
- ♡ 40g (1½oz) caster (superfine) sugar
- ♡ 1.25ml (¼ tsp) gel or paste food colouring (optional)

1 Grease and line baking sheets with baking parchment.

2 Grind the icing (confectioners') sugar and almonds in a food processor to a very fine powder.

3 Using an electric mixer with a large bowl, whisk the egg whites to a foam then add the caster (superfine) sugar gradually and beat until the meringue stands in soft peaks.

4 If making coloured macarons, gently beat in the gel or paste food colouring now.

5 Tip the almond and sugar mixture on top of the meringue. Using a silicone spatula, sweep around the bowl in a circle and then use the blade edge to make rapid sideways strokes ten times.

6 Repeat five more times. The batter should resemble flowing lava. Repeat until it slowly sinks back on itself.

7 Fill a piping (pastry) bag with the batter and pipe the macaron shells onto the lined baking sheets (see Piping macarons in Techniques).

fickle fancies...
Macarons can be temperamental – experiment using different oven shelves or temperatures if you are having problems.

8 Preheat the oven to 150°C/300°F/Gas 2. Leave the trays of shell batter to dry out until a skin forms on each circle – in a warm place this should take around 20 minutes.

9 Bake on a low shelf for 15 minutes. Allow to cool for two minutes then carefully remove from the baking sheets. A few drops of water sprinkled under the paper will steam off any that are stuck.

10 Place on a wire cooling rack and allow to cool completely before making pairs and filling. Enjoy while fresh.

flavour variations

To change the flavour of your macarons, try the following alternatives (you can also use co-ordinating food colourings):

- **Hazelnut:** replace 30g (1oz) ground almonds with 30g (1oz) finely ground hazelnuts and fill with hazelnut spread.

- **Chocolate:** replace 10g (⅜oz) ground almonds with 10g (⅜oz) cocoa powder (unsweetened cocoa).

madeleines

Deceptively sophisticated, these traditional French sponge treats are very easy to make. They taste best fresh from the oven. To get the distinctive shape, you need a Madeleine or mini Madeleine tin (pan). This recipe makes 20 Madeleines or around 48 mini Madeleines.

ingredients...

- ♡ 2 large (US extra large) eggs
- ♡ 90g (3oz) caster (superfine) sugar
- ♡ 100g (3½oz) plain (all-purpose) flour, sifted
- ♡ 2.5ml (½ tsp) baking powder
- ♡ pinch of salt
- ♡ 5ml (1 tsp) vanilla extract
- ♡ 75g (2½oz) unsalted (sweet) butter, melted and cooled plus a little extra for brushing onto the tin (pan)

1 Using an electric mixer with a large bowl, whisk the eggs and sugar together until they have doubled in size and the batter is thick and creamy.
2 Slowly fold in the flour, baking powder and salt taking care not to over mix.

3 Add the vanilla extract then gently fold in the melted butter.
4 Cover the bowl and refrigerate for at least 30 minutes. The batter will be airy and foamy.
5 Preheat the oven to 190°C/375°F/Gas 5 and brush the Madeleine tin (pan) with melted butter.
6 Spoon the batter into the tin (pan), filling each well two-thirds full. If using a mini Madeleine tin (pan), a scant teaspoon of batter will suffice.
7 Bake standard Madeleines for 7 minutes until risen and shrinking away from the edges of the tin (pan). Mini Madeleines need barely 5 minutes – take extra care not to over bake.
8 Allow to cool slightly before turning out onto a wire rack to cool completely.

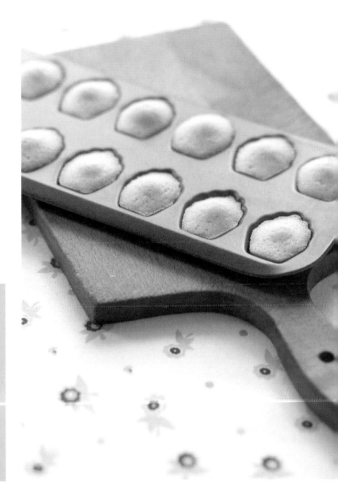

freshness guaranteed...
Madeleine batter can be kept in the fridge for 48 hours so you can bake a few at a time. Stir the chilled batter if it separates. Light when fresh, Madeleines' texture grows sticky and dense within a few hours so enjoy them immediately!

flavour variations

To change the flavour of your Madeleines, try the following alternatives:

- **Orange:** replace the vanilla extract with orange extract and add the finely grated zest of one orange.

- **Lemon and rosemary:** replace the vanilla extract with lemon extract and add 2.5ml (½ tsp) very finely chopped fresh rosemary.

choux pastry

Choux is partially cooked in a saucepan before baking – it is used for éclairs and profiteroles, which are filled with crème patissière (see Fillings and Toppings). This recipe makes around 24 small buns or fingers.

ingredients...

- ♡ 50g (1¾oz) unsalted (sweet) butter
- ♡ 150ml (5fl oz) water
- ♡ pinch of salt
- ♡ 15ml (1 tbsp) caster (superfine) sugar
- ♡ 75g (2½oz) plain (all-purpose) flour, sifted
- ♡ 2 large (US extra large) eggs, beaten
- ♡ 1 large (US extra large) egg for glazing, beaten with a pinch of salt

1 Preheat the oven to 220°C/425°F/Gas 7. Grease and line several baking sheets with baking parchment.

2 Warm the butter, water, salt and sugar in a saucepan then bring to the boil.

3 Reduce the heat and add the flour. Stir quickly until the mixture forms a clean ball of dough.

4 Remove from the heat to cool slightly. Slowly add the eggs, beating well until the mixture stands in soft peaks.

5 Fill a piping (pastry) bag with the warm batter and pipe the buns/fingers onto the baking sheets (see Piping choux buns and fingers in Techniques).

6 Brush the tops with the remaining egg. Bake for 10 minutes until puffed and golden then lower the temperature to180°C/350°F/Gas 4 and bake for a further 15 minutes. The buns should be crisp and dry.

7 On removing from the oven, quickly pierce the side of each bun with a skewer to let the steam out and place on a wire rack to cool.

freshly baked...
Choux buns need to be supremely fresh – don't try to bake them in advance. Once decorated, keep cool but even then they will only stay fresh for a few hours.

sweet pastry

With egg and icing (confectioners') sugar, this sweet pastry is short and light. Keeping everything cool will ensure success but beware of chilling too long as it goes hard quicker than ordinary shortcrust pastry. This recipe makes enough pastry for 20 mini tart cases.

ingredients...

- ♡ 2 egg yolks
- ♡ 20ml (4 tsp) icing (confectioners') sugar, sifted
- ♡ 200g (7oz) plain (all-purpose) flour, sifted, plus extra for rolling out
- ♡ pinch of salt
- ♡ 130g (4½oz) unsalted (sweet) butter, cut into small cubes
- ♡ a little cold water

1 Beat the egg yolks and sugar together in a small bowl.

2 Put the flour and salt in a large bowl, add the butter and rub into a crumb texture with your fingertips.

3 Combine this with the eggs and sugar to make a dough. Add water a few drops at a time to bind the dough.

4 Turn out onto a floured surface and knead lightly until smooth.

5 Wrap in cling film (plastic wrap) and refrigerate for 20–30 minutes before use – no more.

6 Dust the work surface with a little flour and roll out to an even 5mm (³⁄₁₆in) thickness. Cut out as required and bake filled pastry cases at 200°C/400°F/Gas 6 for around 20 minutes in total (see tip).

bake blind...
Small pastry cases will need to be pricked with a fork and 'baked blind' with small squares of parchment paper and baking beans for half the cooking time before filling.

fillings and toppings

vanilla buttercream

This classic topping for cupcakes can also be used to fill macarons or coat fondant fancies before dipping. This quantity is enough to pipe swirls on 18 mini cupcakes or 12 standard or muffin-sized cupcakes, or double that if covered flat with a palette knife. Where buttercream is used in the projects, this recipe makes the quantity needed unless stated otherwise.

ingredients...

- ♡ 80g (2¾oz) unsalted (sweet) butter, softened
- ♡ 250g (8¾oz) icing (confectioners') sugar, sifted
- ♡ up to 30ml (2 tbsp) milk
- ♡ 5ml (1 tsp) vanilla extract
- ♡ gel or paste food colouring (optional)

1 Using an electric mixer with a large bowl, beat the butter until very soft.

2 Gradually beat in the icing (confectioners') sugar.

3 Beat in the milk until you have a soft piping consistency then leave the mixer running a little longer to lighten it further.

4 To add colour, dip a cocktail stick (toothpick) tip into the gel or paste food colouring and swirl into the buttercream. Beat again until the colour is even. Repeat as required.

pipe dreams...
The amount of milk needed to soften buttercream to piping consistency may vary according to the ambient temperature.

flavour variations

To change the flavour of your buttercream, try the following alternatives:

- **Chocolate:** add 40g (1½oz) cocoa powder (unsweetened cocoa) and replace the vanilla extract with chocolate extract.
- **Irish cream:** as for chocolate but replace the milk with Irish cream liqueur.
- **Lemon:** replace half the milk with lemon juice and replace the vanilla extract with lemon extract. Optionally, you can add a few drops of yellow food colouring.

royal icing

This icing dries hard and is used for solid decorations on cakes and cookies. A soft-peak icing can be used to pipe lines whereas a few drops of water will make it runny enough to flood cookies. This recipe yields around 250ml (16½ tbsp) soft-peak icing – enough to cover about 40 cookies, depending on their size and shape.

ingredients...

♡ 1 large (US extra large) egg white

♡ 300g (10½oz) icing (confectioners') sugar, sifted

♡ 10ml (2 tsp) lemon juice

♡ gel or paste food colouring (optional)

1 Using an electric mixer with a large bowl, whisk the egg whites to a light foam.

2 Slowly add the icing (confectioners') sugar then the lemon juice.

3 Beat for up to 10 minutes until you have a soft-peak icing.

4 Add food colouring and/or change the consistency as required for use (see Piping with royal icing in Techniques).

safety first...
For young children and pregnant women, replace raw egg white with meringue powder (sometimes called egg white powder). Manufactured instant royal icing can be useful for smaller quantities.

glacé icing

This soft icing is useful for covering cakes, choux buns and whoopie pies. This recipe makes enough to cover up to 60 small buns or mini whoopie pies.

ingredients...

- ♥ 30ml (2 tbsp) hot water
- ♥ 225g (8oz) icing (confectioners') sugar, sifted
- ♥ gel or paste food colouring (optional)

1 Using a large bowl, gradually add the hot water to the sifted sugar.

2 Stir until smooth. The icing should be thick enough to coat the back of a spoon without dripping off. Adjust the consistency with a little more icing (confectioners') sugar or a few drops of water as necessary.

3 Tint with gel or paste food colouring or flavourings (see flavour variations) as required.

flavour variations

To change the flavour of your glacé icing, try the following alternatives:

- **Coffee:** dissolve 15ml (1 tbsp) instant coffee powder into the hot water before adding to the sugar.
- **Lemon:** add 1.25ml (¼ tsp) lemon extract and a touch of yellow food colouring.

fondant icing

Often called poured fondant, this icing will set firm over a fondant fancy. This recipe covers around 20 fancies, each 4.25cm (1⅝in) square.

ingredients...

- ♡ 750g (1lb 10½oz) icing ('confectioners') sugar, sifted
- ♡ 125ml (4¼fl oz) water
- ♡ 30ml (2 tbsp) golden (corn) syrup
- ♡ gel or paste food colouring (optional)
- ♡ 5ml (1 tsp) vanilla extract or other flavouring as desired

1 Combine the sugar, water and syrup over a low heat in a saucepan stirring continuously. Add colour and flavouring as required.

2 Place a sugar thermometer into the mixture. At 33°C (91°F), the icing should be a pouring consistency but not too thin. Carefully raise the temperature to 45–50°C, (113–122°F) – no higher or the icing will lose its shine.

3 Remove the thermometer probe, if the icing sets hard on the tip of the probe within seconds it is ready.

waste not want not
Fondant icing gives a better finish and is less wasteful when cakes are dipped into it.

chocolate ganache

This luxurious molten chocolate with cream is used for filling, topping and coating cakes. This recipe makes enough to fill around 32 macarons or glaze around 24 mini whoopie pies.

dark/milk chocolate ganache

ingredients...

- 100g (3½oz) dark (semisweet) or milk chocolate, broken into squares
- 100ml (3½fl oz) double (heavy) cream

white chocolate ganache

ingredients...

- 200g (7oz) white chocolate, broken into squares
- 50ml (1¾fl oz) double (heavy) cream

1 Using a double boiler (or a heatproof bowl over a large saucepan), fill the chamber underneath with water just lower than the base. Bring to a gentle simmer.

2 Warm the chocolate and cream in the top of the double boiler, stirring with a wooden spoon as they melt together.

3 Allow to cool sufficiently and use before it sets firm. Refrigerate for up to two weeks. Bring back to room temperature before using.

balancing act...
Adjusting the ratio of cream to chocolate will make thicker or runnier ganache. White chocolate ganache needs a much higher ratio of chocolate to cream otherwise it will not set.

marshmallow fluff

Marshmallow fluff is a thick, white sugary paste used to fill whoopie pies and top red velvet cakes. This recipe makes enough to fill around 24 red velvet hearts or mini whoopies.

ingredients...

- ♡ 1 large (US extra large) egg white
- ♡ 125g (4½oz) caster (superfine) sugar
- ♡ 25g (¾oz) golden (corn) syrup
- ♡ pinch of salt
- ♡ 1.25ml (¼ tsp) cream of tartar
- ♡ 15ml (1 tbsp) water
- ♡ 5ml (1 tsp) vanilla extract

1 Using a double boiler (or a heatproof bowl over a large saucepan), fill the chamber underneath with water just lower than the base. Bring to a simmer.

2 Place the egg white, sugar, syrup, salt, cream of tartar and water in the top of the double boiler.

3 While the mixture heats, use a handheld electric mixer to whisk it. Continue for several minutes until it forms shiny satin peaks.

4 Take the top bowl off the simmering water and whisk for a further two minutes to thicken some more. Beat in the vanilla extract.

5 Cool the fluff before use. It is best used the same day but can be refrigerated for three days. Stir before use if a skin has formed on the surface or if the syrup has sunk to the bottom.

crème patissière

A staple component of French patisserie, 'pastry cream' is used to fill choux buns and fingers. This recipe makes enough to fill around 36 mini choux buns or 30 éclairs.

ingredients...

- ♡ 225ml (8fl oz) milk
- ♡ 5ml (1 tsp) vanilla extract
- ♡ 3 large (US extra large) egg yolks
- ♡ 100g (3½oz) caster (superfine) sugar
- ♡ 15g (½oz) cornflour (cornstarch)
- ♡ 15g (½oz) plain (all-purpose) flour

1 Heat the milk and vanilla in a small saucepan. Bring to the boil and simmer for a few minutes. Turn off the heat and cool for a minute.

2 Meanwhile, whisk the egg yolks and sugar in a large bowl until they are pale then beat in the flours.

3 Whisking continuously, pour over the milk then transfer back to the saucepan. Keep whisking, gently bring back to the boil and simmer for one minute.

4 Turn off the heat and pour into a bowl. Cover with a piece of cling film (plastic wrap) and leave to cool. Chill for several hours or overnight before use. It will keep refrigerated for up to five days.

flavour variations

To change the flavour of your crème patissière, try the following alternatives:

- **Chocolate:** add 75g (2½oz) dark (semisweet) chocolate during the final simmering.
- **Orange:** omit 25ml (1fl oz) milk, replace the vanilla with the zest of one orange and add the juice of half an orange in the final simmering.
- **Lavender:** omit the vanilla extract and replace the caster (superfine) sugar with lavender sugar.

lemon curd filling

This simple but tangy lemon curd is suitable for filling small pastry tarts or whoopie pies. This recipe makes enough to fill around 30 mini tart cases or mini whoopies.

ingredients...

- ♡ 45ml (3 tbsp) cornflour (cornstarch), sifted
- ♡ 75g (2½oz) caster (superfine) sugar
- ♡ grated zest and juice of 3 lemons
- ♡ 225ml (8fl oz) water
- ♡ 3 large (US extra large) egg yolks
- ♡ 50g (1¾oz) unsalted (sweet) butter

1 Mix the cornflour (cornstarch), sugar and lemon zest in a medium-sized bowl. Add a little of the water and mix to a smooth paste.

2 Heat the rest of the water with the lemon juice until just simmering.

3 Mix with the paste and return to the pan.

4 Gradually increase the heat to cook the mixture, stirring continuously until it comes to the boil. Reduce the heat and simmer gently for approximately 3 minutes, stirring all the time.

5 Beat in the egg yolks and butter and cook for a further minute until smooth. The curd thickens as it cools.

techniques

piping with royal icing

With each colour and consistency of royal icing loaded into piping (pastry) bags with the appropriate tubes (tips) before you start, piping will be easier than you think!

you will need...

- ♡ soft-peak royal icing (see Fillings and Toppings)
- ♡ gel or paste food colourings
- ♡ small plastic tubs with lids (one per colour/consistency)
- ♡ piping (pastry) bags
- ♡ no.2 piping tubes (tips)

royal icing piping advice

- Use soft-peak royal icing in a piping (pastry) bag with a no.2 tube (tip) for piping lines and borders on cakes and cookies.
- Make a big batch of soft-peak icing and scoop out smaller quantities to colour as required.
- You can buy re-usable bags with couplers to change tubes (tips) without emptying the bags, but disposable ones are more practical for projects with several bags used at once.
- For fine work with royal icing, small hand-folded bags made from baking parchment (see Step 1) are easier to control and can be unfolded to scrape out leftover icing for re-use.
- Gel or paste food colourings have deeper pigmentation than the liquid varieties sold in supermarkets. Experiment with how pigments behave; a touch of some colours will go a long way whereas red and black may need 2.5ml (½ tsp) or more. Colours can deepen overnight.

1 Cut baking parchment into a neat square and fold diagonally into a triangle. Curl each of the narrow points upwards behind the 90-degree point to create a cone. Fold the paper at the base of the cone over a couple of times to hold it in position.

2 Drop the tube (tip) inside or snip a small hole in the end for the icing to squeeze out.

3 Use two teaspoons to decant the royal icing into the bag. Fold the bag corners inwards and roll upwards to push the icing towards the tube (tip).
4 Hold the tube (tip) between your index and middle finger at a 90 degree angle to the cake. Use your thumb to apply pressure to the bag and push the icing out.

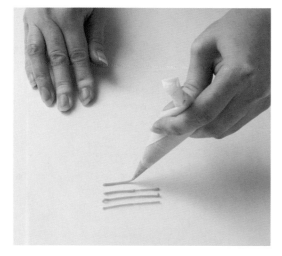

piping straight lines

Keeping the tube (tip) at a 90-degree angle to the work, lift the bag slightly as you squeeze allowing the line of icing to fall where you want it to go.

cut down to size...
Disposable piping (pastry) bags are best trimmed down when working with small quantities of icing.

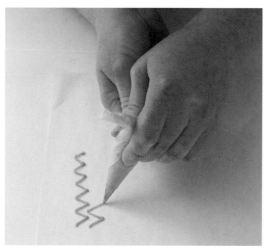

piping zigzags

Keep the tube (tip) closer to the work, touching the surface with the tip before lifting away in the other direction.

piping dots and pearls

Hold the tube (tip) perpendicular to the surface, 1–2mm (1/16in) away from the work as you apply pressure to the bag. Release the pressure before you pull away.

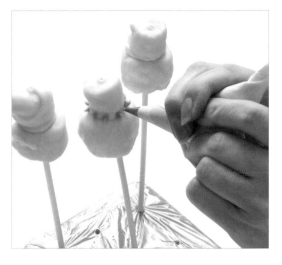

don't be square...
Using pre-cut 23cm (9in) parchment squares is quicker than cutting out your own – better still, they don't curl up!

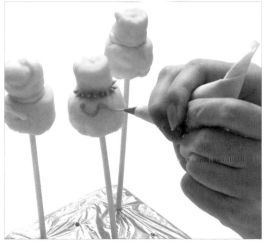

piping loops

Carefully lift the bag away, allowing a longer trail of icing to be expelled before fixing back on the surface.

flooding cookies with royal icing

The sky's the limit when covering cookies with royal icing but preparation and working quickly are key to success. A little water thins royal icing to a flood consistency to fill borders with colour on cookies.

you will need...

- ♡ flood-consistency royal icing (see Fillings and Toppings)
- ♡ gel or paste food colourings
- ♡ small plastic tubs with lids (one per colour/consistency)
- ♡ piping (pastry) bags
- ♡ no.3 piping tubes (tips)
- ♡ cocktail sticks (toothpicks) to spread icing and pop air bubbles

royal icing flooding advice

- Use flood-consistency royal icing in a piping (pastry) bag with a no.3 tube (tip) for flood-filling areas.
- Make a one-egg white quantity of soft-peak white royal icing. As you divide the white icing into each colour and consistency of icing needed for the project, store each type in a separate sealed tub.
- Having as many tubes (tips) and piping (pastry) bags as you have types/colours means you can decorate cookies from start to finish without needing to stop to clean things.
- In the projects, there is always a little extra icing allowed for further mixing — just in case you need more of any colour, which you can tint as required.
- Royal icing will keep for at least one week in airtight containers. Save any leftovers for other projects. If it has gone too stiff to pipe, stir it with a spoon dipped in water — too much water will make it too runny.

flooding bordered areas

Using a piping (pastry) bag filled with flood-consistency icing and fitted with a no.3 tube (tip), squeeze fatter lines of icing inside the piped borders. When filling with the same colour, do so while the thin border is still wet so that the two icings sink into each other. Use a cocktail stick (toothpick) to encourage the icing to fill the space. When filling with a different colour, allow the piped border to dry so the icings stay separate. Colours may bleed if flood icing is too wet.

flood on flood

To create a flat surface in different colours, pipe two colours of flood-consistency icing either next to each other or on top of each other while both are still wet.

feathering

Make stars or streaked effects by feathering two colours of wet flood-consistency icing into one another by pressing a cocktail stick (toothpick) into one colour of wet icing and dragging it into the contrasting coloured area.

piping with buttercream

A soft buttery icing used for topping cupcakes and filling between layers of sponge, buttercream is adaptable enough to take almost any colour or flavour. Large plastic disposable bags are best for piping buttercream, ganache and marshmallow fluff.

you will need...

- ♡ softened buttercream (see Fillings and Toppings)
- ♡ gel or paste food colourings
- ♡ small plastic tubs with lids (one per colour)
- ♡ large piping (pastry) bags
- ♡ piping tubes (tips) – round for spirals, star for swirls and roses, no.98 Tala for clouds

1 To pipe buttercream you can fill the piping (pastry) bag up much more than for finer work with royal icing. Half fill the bag with a tablespoon of icing at a time. Roll the bag partly inside out to avoid wasting icing too far up the bag.

2 The technique for holding the bag is the same as for royal icing (see Piping with royal icing in Techniques). Keep folding the bottom of the bag over to keep the buttercream flowing out as you apply pressure.

piping swirls

Using a star tube (tip), hold the cake in one hand and the bag vertically with the other. Apply pressure to the bag and squeeze with the tip touching the edge of the cake as you turn it and move the tip in a spiral shape finishing the centre.

piping roses

Use the same piping tube (tip) and technique as for swirls, except start in the centre of the cake and work outwards.

piping 'clouds'

Using a no.98 Tala tube (tip), apply pressure to the bag and pull away to leave a bubble of buttercream. Repeat in a circle around the base of the cake then repeat with a second inner circle, and fill any remaining space with a final bubble. This creates a wavy cloud-like effect.

piping choux pastry and macaron shells

If you don't have shaped tubes (tips) here, disposable piping (pastry) bags with the ends snipped off are neat enough to pipe choux pastry or macarons.

piping choux buns and fingers

you will need...

- ♡ warm choux pastry batter (see Recipes)
- ♡ large disposable piping (pastry) bag with 1.5cm (½in) round tube (tip) (or cut with 1cm/⅜in opening)
- ♡ baking sheets lined with baking parchment

1 Fill the piping (pastry) bag two-thirds full with warm choux pastry batter and twist the end to close.

2 With the tip of the bag almost touching the baking sheet, pipe little balls 3cm (1in) wide, 3cm (1in) high and 3cm (1in) apart. The choux puffs up a surprising amount; balls the size of large marbles will rise to profiterole size.

3 To pipe choux fingers, hold the bag with the tube (tip) almost touching the sheet and pipe 5cm (2in) lines of batter looping back on themselves.

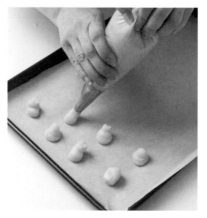

piping macarons

you will need...

- ♡ french macaron batter (see Recipes)
- ♡ large disposable piping (pastry) with 1.5cm (½in) round tube (tip) (or cut with 1cm/⅜in opening)
- ♡ baking sheets lined with baking parchment
- ♡ sheet of A4 paper for piping template

1 Make a template on the sheet of paper by drawing 5cm (2in) circles 4cm (1½in) apart. Slide the template between the baking parchment and the baking sheet.

2 Fill the piping (pastry) bag two-thirds full with macaron batter and twist the end to close. Using the template as a guide, pipe the batter inside the lines in a circular motion ending in the centre with a quick jerk sideways.

3 Once all the macaron shells are piped, remove the template and rap the baking sheet sharply on the work surface to even their surface.

covering cakes with sugarpaste

Sugarpaste (rolled fondant) makes an even, edible covering for either cupcake tops or fondant fancies. It makes an excellent base for further decoration.

you will need...

- ♡ buttercream (see Fillings and Toppings) or warm apricot glaze
- ♡ white sugarpaste
- ♡ gel or paste food colourings
- ♡ icing (confectioners') sugar in a dredger
- ♡ non-stick acrylic mat
- ♡ non-stick miniature rolling pin

1 Prepare the surface of the cake either by covering it with buttercream or brushing it with some warmed apricot glaze.

2 Knead the sugarpaste until nice and pliable. Tint with gel or paste food colouring if required and knead until an even shade is achieved.

keep it clean...
Wearing latex gloves will help avoid staining your hands when working with coloured sugarpaste.

3 Dust the non-stick mat and rolling pin with a little icing (confectioners') sugar and roll out the sugarpaste to an even 3mm (⅛in) thickness into a circle slightly larger than your cake, lifting and turning as you roll to prevent sticking.

4 Carefully place the sugarpaste circle over the cake and press around the shape of the cake with flat fingers (or for larger cakes you can use a cake smoother).

5 Trim the excess icing and patiently smooth over the cut edges with your fingers. Pop any air bubbles with a pin and smooth over.

soft and supple...
Sugar is very drying on your hands, a little white vegetable fat (shortening) will make kneading balls of sugarpaste much easier and help stop it drying out too much before you've finished working with it.

making fondant flowers

With a little time and patience, making impressive-looking sugarpaste roses and blossoms is easier than you think.

you will need...

- ♡ white sugarpaste
- ♡ gel or paste food colourings
- ♡ non-stick acrylic mat
- ♡ non-stick miniature rolling pin
- ♡ daisy and blossom plunger cutters
- ♡ plastic sugarpaste modelling tools
- ♡ A4 plastic sleeve, cut on short edge so it opens like a book
- ♡ lustre powder or liquid
- ♡ small paintbrush

making petalled roses

1 Roll a large grape-sized ball of sugarpaste into a sausage shape. Press to flatten the base and slice into six semicircular pieces.

cut out and keep...
If you make more sugarpaste blooms than you need, you can save them for another day. Once dried, they will keep in an airtight container for months.

2 Arrange the pieces inside the plastic sleeve and apply light pressure to each one with your thumb to flatten the sugarpaste upwards and make petals. The lower edge remains fatter. If they're too thin they will tear when lifted.

3 Remove from the plastic sleeve and roll one of the largest petals into a coiled pointy tube forming the centre of your rose.

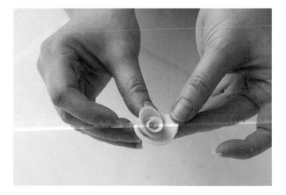

4 Curl a second petal around in the other direction. Then a third. Repeat to build a rose shape squeezing very gently as you go. Arrange the petals with your fingers and slice the base horizontally to leave a small rose.

5 To finish, apply lustre powder or liquid with a small brush. Sugarpaste roses can be used immediately but if you dry them for a few hours they are less liable to be squashed when putting them into place on your cakes.

making spiral roses

1 Take a grape-sized ball of sugarpaste, position inside the plastic sleeve and flatten with the ball of your hand and thumb until the circle is around 8cm (3in) in diameter.

2 Open the sleeve and cut the flat circle vertically into three strips. Take the outer strips and coil into tight spirals. Use your fingers to shape and cut the base and finish as for petalled roses (see Making petalled roses in Techniques). Repeat with the centre strip.

using a plunger cutter

Plunger cutters come in daisy and blossom shapes. Use them to punch out shapes from rolled sugarpaste. Keep the insides of the cutters clean and dry, as the sugary residue from old shapes can cause paste to get stuck. Sugarpaste daisies are especially fragile so let these dry out and handle them very carefully, taking care not to snap the petals. Pipe the centres with royal icing.

piping leaves

Although you can get plunger cutters or moulds to make leaves, a convincing delicate leaf can be piped from royal icing using a piping (pastry) bag with a small 'V' shape snipped in the end. Little spiral roses look especially good affixed to green royal icing leaves. This technique can also be used to make chocolate ganache leaves on coffee profiteroles (see Café Crème in Petit Fours).

Hold the tip of the bag just touching the surface and squeeze gently with your thumb allowing icing to build up. Wiggle the point from side to side as you pull away upwards leaving a leaf shape. Depending on the project, you can pipe these leaves directly onto cakes or onto baking parchment ready to affix to flowers and cakes when dry.

making fondant novelties

Sugarpaste can be used to model novelties and shapes for the tops of your cakes. It is edible and upon drying keeps its shape without going too hard. You can buy coloured sugarpaste but more individual colours can be easily achieved by tinting it yourself.

you will need...

- ♡ white sugarpaste
- ♡ gel or paste food colourings
- ♡ non-stick acrylic mat
- ♡ non-stick miniature rolling pin
- ♡ metal or plunger cutters
- ♡ small palette knife
- ♡ baking parchment
- ♡ plastic sugarpaste modelling tools
- ♡ lustre power or metallic lustre spray
- ♡ royal icing

1 Knead a ball of sugarpaste the size of a small orange until it is soft. Using a cocktail stick (toothpick) add gel or paste food colouring to the ball and knead until evenly spread. Repeat to get the desired shade.

2 Roll out the sugarpaste on a non-stick mat with a non-stick rolling pin. Using metal or plunger cutters, cut out shapes and lift carefully from the mat with a small palette knife and transfer to a sheet of baking parchment. Rub any rough edges carefully with your fingers to smooth out. Use the modelling tools to make indentations or any curling effects.

3 Affix pieces of cut sugarpaste together with a dot of royal icing; when assembled, brush over with lustre powder or spray with metallic lustre spray. Position on your cakes as required.

making small bows

Roll out a grape-sized ball of sugarpaste to an even 3mm (⅛in) thickness. Trim into ribbons 6mm (¼in) wide and 4cm (1½in) long. Fold the outer edges in towards the centre to make the top part of bow and use another piece to make ties and a knot. Use the comb tool to mark stitches.

making gift bows

Use the same technique as for small bows but create more 4cm (1½in) long ribbons. Fold into a loop and flatten at one end. Repeat nine times, making half of the loops a bit smaller than the others. Cut out a 3cm (1in) circle and mount the larger loops with the flat ends at the centre with small loops on top. Fix the pieces together with dots of royal icing.

making and dipping fondant fancies

Fondant fancies comprise a sponge centre, a layer of marzipan and a fondant icing coating. They're often square and coloured pink, yellow or brown but are crying out to be as versatile as cupcakes. Two pairs of hands are useful to dip and turn fancies over without smudging them. The method below is a little unorthodox but you can always get a friend to help instead!

you will need...

- ♡ 20cm (8in) sponge cake
- ♡ 300g (10½oz) marzipan
- ♡ 200g (7oz) apricot glaze, warmed
- ♡ silicone brush
- ♡ baking sheet or tray to place cakes in freezer
- ♡ ruler
- ♡ bread knife
- ♡ wire cooling rack
- ♡ 4 baked bean tins – or an extra pair of hands!
- ♡ fondant icing (see Fillings and Toppings)
- ♡ cocktail sticks (toothpicks) or a candy dipping tool

1 Bake your fancies according to the type required for the project, either using moulds or as a 20cm (8in) square cake.

2 If using a large square cake, brush the top surface with warmed apricot glaze and cover with a 3mm (⅛in) layer of marzipan. Place the cake in the freezer for 10 minutes.

3 Remove from the freezer and using a cocktail stick (toothpick) and a ruler, mark out a 17cm (6¾in) square centrally on the cake. Trim the sides with a bread knife. Plot more lines with the cocktail stick (toothpick) and cut the cake into 16 smaller squares (four rows of four), each 4.25cm (1⅝in) square.

4 Return the cakes to the freezer for 10 minutes while you make the fondant icing. Chillled, firmed cakes are easier to handle and make a warm coating set quicker.

5 Raise your wire cooling rack by placing four baked bean tins underneath, one in each corner.

6 Remove the cakes from the freezer and the fondant icing from the heat and spear each cake with two cocktail sticks (toothpicks) at 45-degree angles into the base. Swirl upside down in the fondant icing then turn right side up allowing the excess icing to drip off.

keep it simple...
A simpler covering for fancies is melted chocolate or sugarpaste (see Covering cakes with sugarpaste in Techniques).

7 Place the cake on the raised wire rack and pull the cocktail sticks out from underneath.

8 If the fondant icing dries or clumps you need to return it to the heat briefly before continuing.

making cake pops

Easy and fun to make, cake balls or 'pops' on a stick are a great way to use up pieces of sponge left over from other projects. This recipe makes around 20 cake pops, depending on their shape and size. Candy Melts are perfect for dipping and a little added white vegetable fat (shortening) creates a better consistency for swirling.

you will need...

♡ 300g (10½oz) sponge cake (see Recipes)

♡ 150g (5½oz) softened buttercream (see Fillings and Toppings)

♡ 400g (14oz) Candy Melts (see Suppliers)

♡ up to 75g (2½oz) white vegetable fat (shortening)

♡ baking parchment

♡ lollipop sticks

♡ florists' oasis block wrapped in cling film (plastic wrap) or polystyrene block

♡ double boiler or plastic microwave saucepan (or even a mug in the microwave)

1 In a large bowl, crumble the sponge with your fingers. Lightly rub in the softened buttercream in a similar manner to making shortcrust pastry until you can squeeze balls from the mix.

2 With your fingers, roll golf-ball sized balls from the mixture. Lay on a piece of baking parchment on a plate or tray and freeze for 10 minutes.

3 Melt the Candy Melts and add shavings of white vegetable fat (shortening) until the mixture is the consistency of low-fat

yoghurt. Dip 3cm (1in) of each lollipop stick end into the mixture and push into the base of each cake ball to fix it onto the stick.

4 Holding the lollipop stick end, swirl the ball around in the Candy Melts mixture. Use a cocktail stick (toothpick) to help cover any missed bits and allow the excess to drizzle away.

5 While wet, dip in sprinkles as desired or allow to dry before piping a design in royal icing.

6 Push the sticks into the oasis or polystyrene block to dry.

easier dipping...
This quantity of Candy Melts will make much more than you need to cover the cake pops, however it is infinitely easier to use a generous bowlful than a shallow one.

projects

chocolate drizzles

These classic chocolate-coated fancies might look like big truffles but they hide a chocolate sponge layered with jam and buttercream.

you will need...

- ♡ chocolate sponge baked as 18 round cannelles, or 20cm (8in) cake cut into 16 squares
- ♡ 150g (5¼oz) smooth blackcurrant or cherry jam
- ♡ chocolate buttercream
- ♡ 200g (7oz) milk chocolate
- ♡ 5ml (1 tsp) white vegetable fat (shortening)
- ♡ 90ml (6 tbsp) dark brown soft-peak royal icing
- ♡ piping (pastry) bag with no.3 tube (tip)
- ♡ candy dipping tool

1 Place the cakes on a parchment-lined baking sheet and freeze for 10 minutes. If using a cannelle mould, slice the bases flat.

2 Remove from the freezer, slice horizontally and sandwich back together with a little jam. If you can, leave the cakes overnight – the jam soaks in and they're sturdier when dipped.

3 Cover tops of the cakes with a disc of buttercream, Return to the freezer for 10 more minutes.

4 Meanwhile, using a double boiler (or a large heatproof bowl over a saucepan of water), melt the chocolate with shavings of white vegetable fat (shortening) and allow to cool slightly.

5 When the cakes are cold and firm, pierce the fancy with one prong of the candy dipping tool and submerge in the melted chocolate. Use a cocktail stick (toothpick) to smooth the surface and place on a wire rack to set.

6 Fill the piping (pastry) bag with dark brown royal icing and pipe spirals or zigzags onto the cakes.

break the mould...
These round fancies have been baked in a cannelle mould. Alternatively you could cut a large cake into squares or circles.

recipes chocolate sponge cake, chocolate buttercream, royal icing

techniques piping with royal icing

orange blossoms

Orange flavour comes from the sponge, the marmalade and the icing for these blossomed fancies, giving a refreshing citrus hit.

you will need...

- ♡ 20cm (8in) square sponge flavoured with orange extract
- ♡ 200g (7oz) shredless marmalade, warmed
- ♡ 300g (10½oz) marzipan
- ♡ fondant icing, flavoured with 2.5ml (½ tsp) orange flower water and tinted pale orange
- ♡ 90ml (6 tbsp) pale green soft-peak royal icing
- ♡ sugarpaste: 200g (7oz) pale orange
- ♡ disposable piping (pastry) bag
- ♡ 16 muffin-sized paper cupcake cases

1 Brush the top of the cake with warmed marmalade and cover with a 3mm (⅛in) layer of marzipan. Place the cake in the freezer for 10 minutes.

2 Remove from the freezer and cut into 16 squares.

3 Place the fancies on a baking sheet lined with baking parchment and freeze for a further 10 minutes while you heat the fondant icing to the correct temperature and consistency.

4 When the cakes are cold and firm, dip into the fondant icing and place on a wire rack to set.

5 Roll out the pale orange sugarpaste and model 16 petalled roses, cutting them close to their bases. Set aside.

6 Fill the piping (pastry) bag with the pale green royal icing and cut a 3mm (⅛in) 'V'-shape in the end of the bag. Pressure pipe pairs of green leaves onto baking parchment. Press a sugarpaste rose onto each pair of leaves and allow to dry.

7 When the leaves have dried, carefully lift each flower and affix them to the top of the fancies with a dot of green royal icing. Serve in the paper cases, pinching them at the corners to square them off and stand the cakes close together.

---

recipes sponge cake, royal icing, fondant icing

techniques piping with royal icing, making fondant flowers, piping leaves, making and dipping fondant fancies

all wrapped up

Some presents are wrapped so beautifully that it's a shame to open them ... or in this case, eat them!

you will need...

- ♡ 20cm (8in) square vanilla sponge
- ♡ 200g (7oz) apricot glaze, warmed
- ♡ 300g (10½oz) marzipan
- ♡ fondant icing, tinted pale green
- ♡ sugarpaste: 300g (10½oz) white
- ♡ 30–45ml (2–3 tbsp) white soft-peak royal icing
- ♡ piping (pastry) bag with no.2 tube (tip)
- ♡ 16 muffin-sized paper cupcake cases

1 Brush the top of the cake with warmed apricot glaze and cover with a 3mm (⅛in) layer of marzipan. Place the cake in the freezer for 10 minutes.

2 Remove from the freezer and cut into 16 squares.

3 Place the fancies on a baking sheet lined with baking parchment and freeze for a further 10 minutes while you heat the fondant icing to the correct temperature and consistency.

4 When the cakes are cold and firm, dip into the warm fondant icing and place on a wire rack.

5 Roll out the white sugarpaste to an even 3mm (⅛in) thickness and shape into 16 miniature gift bows.

6 With a dot of royal icing, affix the bows on top of the cakes. Serve in the paper cases, pinching them at the corners to square them off and stand the cakes close together.

tie it together... Instead of making 3D fondant bows, try piping string and bows directly onto the cakes with white royal icing.

recipes vanilla sponge cake, royal icing, fondant icing

techniques making fondant novelties, making and dipping fondant fancies

heavenly handbags

If you covet designer handbags, you can enjoy these little quilted fancies without having to go on a lengthy waiting list!

you will need...

- ♡ 16 sponge rectangles, 3 x 4cm (1⅛ x 1½in) (offcuts from other projects)
- ♡ 200g (7oz) apricot glaze, warmed
- ♡ 100g (3½oz) vanilla buttercream
- ♡ sugarpaste: 500g (1lb) tinted purple, pink, and/or left white (allow 30g/1oz per bag), 25g (⅞oz) pale brown
- ♡ gold and silver lustre liquid
- ♡ 15ml (1 tbsp) pale brown soft-peak royal icing
- ♡ piping (pastry) bag with no.2 tube (tip)
- ♡ comb and pointed modelling tools

1 Brush warm apricot glaze on the cake tops, cover the top with a small blob of buttercream and smooth the surface.

2 Place the cakes on a baking sheet lined with parchment and freeze for 10 minutes.

3 When the cakes are cold and firm, brush the sides with apricot glaze. Roll out a plum-sized ball of sugarpaste to 12cm (4¾in) diameter, cover the cake and rub the edges smooth.

4 Use the comb tool to press a grid pattern of stitch lines into the sugarpaste.

5 Roll out a marble-sized ball of sugarpaste in the same

colour into a square as wide as the long edge of the cake. Press this onto the top for the handbag flap and press on stitching lines before.

6 For the handle, roll the same colour of sugarpaste into a 4cm (1½in) sausage and bend into a horseshoe shape. Roll some pale brown sugarpaste into three small ovals and impress with the pointed tool. Paint with lustre liquid and leave to dry.

7 Pipe dots of pale brown royal icing to stick an oval to each end of the handle. Leave to dry then fix the handle to the bag and add an extra oval for the clasp.

recipes sponge cake, vanilla buttercream, royal icing

techniques piping with royal icing, covering cakes with sugarpaste, making fondant novelties

'tis the season

For those who dislike fruit cake or prefer a lighter alternative, these miniature red velvet fancies are a delicate festive treat.

you will need...

- ♥ 20cm (8in) red velvet cake, cut into 16 squares
- ♥ 300g (10½oz) marzipan
- ♥ 200g (7oz) apricot glaze, warmed
- ♥ sugarpaste: 1kg (2¼lb) white
- ♥ mini snowflake plunger cutter
- ♥ silver lustre dust
- ♥ soft-peak royal icing: 25% green, 25% red, 50% white
- ♥ 4 piping (pastry) bags, 1 with no.2 tube (tip), 3 with no.3 tubes (tips)

for the holly fancies

1 Pipe holly leaf shapes 1.5cm (½in) in length onto parchment using green icing in a bag with a no.2 tube (tip).

2 Place the cakes on a baking sheet and freeze for 10 minutes.

3 Roll out the marzipan to 0.5cm (¼in) thick and cut out squares the same size as the cakes.

4 Smear warmed apricot glaze on the cakes and fix the marzipan on top.

5 Roll out a plum-sized ball of sugarpaste to a 15cm (6in) circle. Cover the cake and rub the edges smooth. Repeat for the other cakes.

6 Using the bag from step 1, pipe dots on the top of each fancy and attach two or three dry piped leaves.

7 Pipe berries on the leaves with red icing in a bag with a no.3 tube (tip).

8 Pipe red dots around the base of each fancy, leaving room for green dots in between. Transfer the green icing to a bag with a no.3 tube (tip) and pipe dots in the spaces.

for the snowflake fancies

1 Cover the cakes with white sugarpaste. Cut mini snowflakes from the trimmings with a plunger cutter and brush with silver lustre dust.

2 Pipe a dot on top of each fancy with white royal icing in a bag with a no.3 tube (tip) and attach the snowflakes. Pipe dots around the bases and lines around the sides.

recipes red velvet cake, royal icing

techniques piping with royal icing, covering cakes with sugarpaste, piping leaves, making and dipping fondant fancies

baby shower

These adorable baby faces with pink or blue hats for boys or girls are perfect for a baby shower or christening party.

you will need...

- ♡ 32 mini vanilla cupcakes baked in pink or blue paper cases
- ♡ vanilla buttercream
- ♡ sugarpaste: 150g (5¼oz) each pale pink or blue and beige
- ♡ chopstick
- ♡ comb modelling tool
- ♡ 45ml (3 tbsp) each mid blue or pink, and dark brown soft-peak royal icing
- ♡ 2 piping (pastry) bags with no.2 tubes (tips)
- ♡ mini easter egg cutter
- ♡ 1cm (⅜in) round cutter

1 Roll out the beige sugarpaste to an even 2mm (¹⁄₁₆in) thickness and cut out 32 mini easter egg shapes. Repeat with the blue or pink sugarpaste. Also in blue or pink, cut out 1cm (⅜in) circles to use as dummies (pacifiers).

2 Using the easter egg cutter, trim away the pointy end of the blue or pink egg shapes leaving hat shapes.

3 Make stitch marks with the comb modelling tool. Affix hats to the beige faces with water.

4 With the end of a chopstick, impress nostrils and eyes onto the faces. Affix the dummies (pacifiers) with a dab of water.

5 Using mid blue or pink royal icing, pipe pompoms and ribbing on the hats and loops on the dummies (pacifiers).

6 Pipe dots of brown royal icing to fill the eyeholes. Allow to dry.

7 Using a small palette knife, spread a coating of buttercream on top of the cupcakes. Use a little royal icing to fix the baby faces to each cupcake.

baby booties ...
For booties roll a bean-size ball of sugarpaste, top with a flattened pea-sized ball and indent with a ball modelling tool

recipes vanilla sponge cake, vanilla buttercream, royal icing
techniques piping with royal icing, making fondant novelties

sporty balls

No matter what sport they're into, the balls can be depicted with these cupcakes. Perfect for Father's Day or an older boy's birthday.

you will need...

- ♡ 32 mini chocolate cupcakes baked in green foil cases
- ♡ 100g (3½oz) apricot glaze, warmed
- ♡ sugarpaste: 200g (7oz) each white, lime green and mid brown
- ♡ small bone and spear modelling tools
- ♡ 30ml (2 tbsp) each white, dark brown and red soft-peak royal icing
- ♡ 3 piping (pastry) bags with no.2 tubes (tips)
- ♡ 5cm (2in) round cutter

1 Brush the tops of the cakes with warmed apricot glaze. Set aside.

2 Roll out the sugarpastes to a even 2mm (¹⁄₁₆in) thickness and cut out 5cm (2in) circles in all three colours, until you have 64 circles.

3 Press the sugarpaste circles gently onto the cupcake tops and smooth towards the edge of the cases. Apply a second layer to get a round domed top.

4 For the tennis balls Pipe a wavy line of white royal icing onto the lime green cakes.

5 For the baseballs Pipe two lines of red royal icing onto the white cakes in a herringbone pattern.

6 For the basketballs Pipe lines of dark brown royal icing onto the mid-brown cakes in a crisscross pattern.

7 For the golf balls Make rows of indentations on the white cakes with the small bone tool.

8 For the soccer balls Mark lines on the surface of the white cakes with a spear tool.

cracking up...
Sugarpaste shapes quickly crack if left exposed – work with a few circles at a time and cover the rest with an acrylic mat.

recipes chocolate sponge cake, royal icing
techniques piping with royal icing

over the rainbow

Fluffy clouds of buttercream hide striking layers of rainbow sponge.

you will need...

- ♡ vanilla sponge batter (unbaked)
- ♡ mini muffin tins (pans) lined with 32 red foil cases
- ♡ green, blue, yellow and red gel or paste food colourings
- ♡ sugarpaste: 100g (3½oz) orange, 50g (1¾oz) each red, yellow, green and blue
- ♡ vanilla buttercream
- ♡ piping (pastry) bag with no.98 Tala tube (tip)
- ♡ gold lustre liquid
- ♡ spear modelling tool (or small knife)
- ♡ 8mm (¼in) star cutter

1 Divide the cake batter into four equal quantities and tint with each of the four food colourings.
2 Using teaspoons, spoon a little blue, green then yellow and red batters into the paper cases. Bake as normal (see Vanilla sponge cake in Recipes) and cool on a wire rack.
3 Take half of the orange sugarpaste, roll out to an even 2mm (⅟₁₆in) thickness and cut out 64 stars. Brush with gold lustre liquid and leave to dry.
4 Meanwhile, roll little sausages of each sugarpaste colour. Gradually reduce them to the width of cooked spaghetti. Line strips of the colours up to form a

rainbow, flatten slightly with your rolling pin. Trim and shape into arcs and set aside to dry.
5 Using a piping (pastry) bag fitted with a no.98 Tala tube (tip), pipe 'clouds' of buttercream onto the cupcakes to give a bubbly, cloud effect.
6 To finish, press one rainbow and two stars into the soft buttercream on each cake.

up and away...
As a quick alternative, use a mini easter egg cutter to cut pairs of sugarpaste balloons. Position in the clouds and pipe dark brown strings.

recipes vanilla sponge cake, vanilla buttercream
techniques piping with buttercream, making fondant novelties

raspberry kisses

Fresh raspberry in the buttercream gives these mini cupcakes a fruity flavour that will make everyone want to pucker up!

you will need...

- ♡ 32 mini vanilla cupcakes baked in pink foil cases
- ♡ sugarpaste: 250g (8¾oz) pink
- ♡ spear modelling tool
- ♡ pale pink lustre spray
- ♡ 30g (1oz) fresh raspberries
- ♡ buttercream
- ♡ pale pink gel or paste food colouring
- ♡ piping (pastry) bag with 1.5cm (½in) star tube (tip)
- ♡ 60g (2oz) icing (confectioners') sugar

1 Make marble-sized balls from pink sugarpaste, roll into a barrel shape then form soft points at each end. Divide into pairs of lips.

2 Using the spear modelling tool, indent the centre of each top lip and stroke lines outwards. Squeeze the lips together into a pout.

3 Spray the lips with pale pink lustre spray and leave to dry.

4 Meanwhile, tint the buttercream with the pale pink food colouring then crush the raspberries into the buttercream until completely mixed. As they release juice, add extra icing (confectioners') sugar to return the buttercream to piping consistency.

5 Fill the piping (pastry) bag with the raspberry buttercream and pipe swirls on top of the cupcakes.

6 To finish, push the fondant lips into position.

get fruity...
For an extra burst of berry, pop half a raspberry into each case of cupcake batter before baking.

recipes vanilla sponge cake, buttercream
techniques piping with buttercream, making fondant novelties

ladies day

Whether it's a trip to the races or granny's birthday, even ladies who don't wear hats can still enjoy them on cupcakes!

you will need...

- ♡ 32 mini vanilla cupcakes baked in gold foil cases
- ♡ sugarpaste: 250g (8¾oz) each pink and purple
- ♡ ball modelling tool
- ♡ 30–45ml (2–3 tbsp) yellow soft-peak royal icing
- ♡ 2 piping (pastry) bags, 1 with no.2 tube (tip), 1 with 1.5cm (½in) star tube (tip)
- ♡ pale pink lustre spray
- ♡ 7mm (¼in) blossom plunger cutter
- ♡ vanilla buttercream
- ♡ pink coloured sugar

1 Form grape-sized balls of pink and purple sugarpaste. Slice each one into two half spheres.

2 Roll one half into a flat disc measuring 4cm (1½in) across for the brim of the hat.

3 With the other piece, use the ball modelling tool to shape indentations in the hat top.

4 Using a dab of royal icing on the underside, affix the top slightly to one side on the brim.

5 Curve the brim by folding the wider side upwards then spray the hats lightly with pale pink lustre spray and allow to dry.

6 Using a blossom plunger cutter, cut out 32 miniature blossom shapes from the leftover purple and pink sugarpastes.

7 Using a piping (pastry) bag with a no.2 tube (tip), pipe tiny dots of yellow royal icing into the centre of each blossom and around the ribbon line of each hat. Use a dot of royal icing to affix blossoms to each hat. Allow to dry.

8 Using a piping (pastry) bag with 1.5cm (½in) star tube (tip), pipe swirls of buttercream onto the cupcakes.

9 Sprinkle the cupcakes with the pink coloured sugar then gently push the hats onto the top of the buttercream swirls.

recipes vanilla sponge cake, vanilla buttercream, royal icing
techniques piping with royal icing, piping with buttercream, making fondant novelties

so Cosmopolitan

Bring out your inner Carrie Bradshaw with this cookie tribute to the classic Cosmopolitan cocktail.

you will need...

- ♡ 15 cocktail glass cookies and 15 cocktail shaker cookies (see Templates)
- ♡ soft-peak royal icing: 20% white, 20% pink, 20% grey, 10% green, 10% black, 20% reserved for further mixing as required
- ♡ 8 piping (pastry) bags, 4 with no.2 tubes (tips), 4 with no.3 tubes (tips)
- ♡ cocktail sticks (toothpicks)
- ♡ pink sugar crystals

NB Use a piping (pastry) bag with a no.2 tube (tip) and soft-peak icing to pipe the lines in this project. Flood the cookies using flood-consistency icing (add a few drops of water to the soft-peak icing) using a bag with a no.3 tube (tip).

for the cocktail glasses

1 Pipe a triangle of pink icing inside the glass then flood the centre with pink flood icing.

2 Pipe a circle of green icing on one corner of the glass. Mix a little pale green flood icing from green and white and fill the circle. Using a cocktail stick (toothpick), quickly feather darker green icing into the

flooded area for lime slices. Leave to set.

3 Pipe the outline of the glass in white icing. While wet, sprinkle pink sugar crystals on the top edge of the glass. Allow to dry.

for the cocktail shakers

1 Pipe outlines in black and allow to set.

2 When dry, fill with grey flood icing and immediately highlight with blobs of white flood icing. Allow to set.

shaken not stirred...
Use the same glass shape to make a Martini cocktail cookie with a piped olive.

---

recipes vanilla cookies, royal icing

techniques piping with royal icing, flooding cookies with royal icing

bring out the bunting

Nothing creates a party atmosphere like a string of bunting. This edible version is perfect to hang over your party table.

you will need...

- ♡ vanilla cookie dough
- ♡ wooden skewer
- ♡ soft-peak royal icing: 25% blue, 25% red, 25% white, 25% for mixing further colours as required (double the recipe quantity)
- ♡ 6 piping (pastry) bags, 3 with no.2 tubes (tips), 3 with no.3 tubes (tips)
- ♡ 5m (5½yd) ribbon or raffia tape

1 Preheat the oven to 180°C/350°F/ Gas 4. Roll out the dough to 0.75cm (¼in) thick and cut into strips 8cm (3in) wide. Cut the strips into 40–50 triangles, each 6cm (2½in) wide.

2 Using a skewer, make a hole in each cookie, centrally 1.5cm (½in) in from the wide edge.

3 Place the triangles at least 4cm (1½in) apart on a lined baking sheet and bake for 10 minutes.

4 Remove and immediately widen the holes with the skewer. Allow to cool for a moment before transferring to a wire rack to cool completely.

5 Place 60ml (4 tbsp) soft-peak icing in each colour in a piping (pastry) bag with a no.2 tube (tip).

6 Transfer the rest of the soft-peak icing into tubs and gradually add water until you have flood-consistency icing. Place 45ml (3 tbsp) of each colour in a bag with a no.3 tube (tip).

7 Pipe lines around the edges of the cookies with soft-peak icing. Allow to set then fill in with flood icing.

8 Pipe spots of flood icing in a contrasting colour and allow to dry.

9 Leaving 1m (1yd) at each end, thread the ribbon through a cookie. Loop it back through the hole and gently pull taut. Continue spacing the triangles 15cm (6in) apart, keeping them facing the same way. Tie the ends in bows ready to hang up.

recipes vanilla cookies, royal icing
techniques piping with royal icing, flooding cookies with royal icing

skeleton treats

In Mexico, 31 October is the 'day of the dead', a feast day when families believe the spirits of their deceased relatives return. Decorated skull characters often feature in the celebrations.

you will need...

- ♡ 40 gingerbread skull cookies (see Templates)
- ♡ soft-peak royal icing: 30% white, 15% black, 15% pink, 15% yellow, 15% blue, 10% reserved for further mixing as required
- ♡ silver sugar baubles
- ♡ 7 piping (pastry) bags, 5 with no.2 tubes (tips), 2 with no.3 tubes (tips)

NB Use a piping (pastry) bag with a no.2 tube (tip) and soft-peak icing to pipe the lines and details in this project. Flood the cookies using flood-consistency icing (add a few drops of water to the soft-peak icing) using a bag with a no.3 tube (tip).

1 Take half of the white royal icing and make it flood consistency.

2 Pipe white outlines around the edges of the skull cookies and pea-sized circles for the eye sockets.

3 Immediately fill the faces of the skulls with white flood icing. While wet, affix a silver bauble to each side of each skull and leave to set.

4 Pipe tiny black streaks for nostrils and a crisscross line for the mouth. Fill the eye sockets with a large dot of black flood icing.

5 Pipe pink, yellow and blue flower details on the foreheads, cheeks, chins and temples of the skulls.

harem scarem...
If you skip the floral details and baubles, these cookies become suitably scary goodies for Halloween trick or treaters.

recipes gingerbread cookies, royal icing
techniques piping with royal icing, flooding cookies with royal icing

dress to impress

Inspired by iconic outfits worn by Marilyn Monroe and Audrey Hepburn, these dressy little cookies are stars in their own right.

you will need...

- ♡ 32 dress cookies (see Templates)
- ♡ soft-peak royal icing: 40% bright pink, 40% black, 10% white, 10% reserved for further mixing as required
- ♡ silver sugar pearls or baubles
- ♡ silver lustre dust
- ♡ 5 piping (pastry) bags, 3 with no.2 tubes (tip), 2 with no.3 tubes (tips)

NB Use a piping (pastry) bag with a no.2 tube (tip) and soft-peak icing to pipe the lines and dots in this project. Flood the cookies using flood-consistency icing (add a few drops of water to the soft-peak icing) using a bag with a no.3 tube (tip).

1 Take two-thirds each of the pink and black icings and make them flood consistency.

2 For 'Marilyn' Pipe outlines of pink icing around the dress shape with a straight edge above the bust area. At the base, pipe an inverted open loop as a side slit.

3 Fill the cookie with pink flood icing and allow to set. When dry, pipe pink details on the waist and hip.

4 For the necklace, pipe dots of white royal icing around the neck and, while wet, press on silver sugar baubles. Using a very fine paintbrush, brush silver lustre dust on any exposed white icing of the necklace. Make 16 Marilyn cookies.

5 For 'Audrey' Repeat the process with black icing, piping a shift-dress neckline and seam details on the bust, hip and lower skirt as shown.

6 For the necklace, pipe dots and press on one silver bauble at the centre. Make 16 Audrey cookies.

soft and sweet... Sugar pearls are softer than hard metallic sugar baubles.

recipes vanilla cookies, royal icing

techniques piping with royal icing, flooding cookies with royal icing

surf's up

Play with different icing techniques here to create glossy surfboards and leafy palm trees that will instantly conjure memories of the beach.

you will need...

- ♡ 20 surfboard cookies and 12 palm tree cookies (see Templates)
- ♡ soft-peak royal icing: 20% green, 20% orange, 20% bright blue, 10% pale brown, 10% dark brown, 20% reserved for further mixing as required
- ♡ 10 piping (pastry) bags, 5 with no.2 tubes (tips), 5 with no.3 tubes (tips)

NB Use a piping (pastry) bag with a no.2 tube (tip) and soft-peak icing to pipe the lines in this project. Flood the cookies using flood-consistency icing (add a few drops of water to the soft-peak icing) using a bag with a no.3 tube (tip).

for the palm trees

1 Pipe outlines of green icing for the leaves and dark brown for the trunks with angled sections in the bark. Allow to dry.

2 Fill the trunks with pale brown and the leaves with green flood icing. Allow to dry.

3 Pipe green icing around the border and in parallel lines on each leaf.

for the surfboards

1 Pipe one half the border with orange icing and the other with bright blue icing.

2 While wet, pipe orange flood icing inside one half and bright blue flood icing in the other.

3 Working quickly, pipe contrasting flooded dots on one side and streak a wave effect down the centre with a cocktail stick (toothpick).

wipe out...
If it all goes horribly wrong, scrape the icing off and start again. The new icing should cover any earlier mistakes.

recipes chocolate cookies, royal icing

techniques piping with royal icing, flooding cookies with royal icing

ballerina dreams

This design only uses two types of icing but needs a steady hand to sketch delicate ballet shoes onto plain cookies.

you will need...

- ♡ 32 gingerbread cookies, 7cm (2¾in) square
- ♡ soft-peak royal icing: 40% ivory, 40% dusky pink, 20% reserved for further mixing as required
- ♡ 2 piping (pastry) bags, 1 with no.2 tube (tip), 1 with no.3 tube (tip)
- ♡ Piping template (see Templates)

NB Use a piping (pastry) bag with a no.2 tube (tip) and soft-peak icing to pipe the lines and details in this project. Flood the cookies using flood-consistency icing (add a few drops of water to the soft-peak icing) using a bag with a no.3 tube (tip).

1 Using ivory icing and referring to the template as a visual aid, pipe the outlines of the ballet shoes, lower legs and ribbons. Allow to set.

2 Make the dusky pink icing flood consistency and flood the shoe and ribbon areas. Allow to set.

3 Finally, pipe a tiny ivory bow on the front of each shoe.

practice makes perfect...
Try piping the design onto baking parchment a few times first before you tackle your cookies. Getting the icing to flow at just the right speed is key.

en pointe...
If freehand piping is too nerve-wracking, spike dots with a cocktail stick (toothpick) through the template onto the raw cookies before baking.

recipes gingerbread cookies, royal icing
techniques piping with royal icing, flooding cookies with royal icing

delicious dominos

If you get your spots right you can play a real game of dominos before you eat these cookies!

you will need...

- 28 chocolate cookies, 3 x 7cm (1 x 2¾in) (half the recipe quantity)
- soft-peak royal icing: 70% ivory, 15% dark brown, 15% reserved for further mixing as required
- 3 piping (pastry) bags, 2 with no.2 tubes (tips), 1 with no.3 tube (tip)

1 Take around two-thirds of the ivory icing and make it flood consistency by adding a few drops of water to the soft-peak icing.

2 Using a bag with a no.2 tube (tip), pipe a border around each rectangle with ivory icing then immediately flood inside each border with ivory flood icing in a bag with a no.3 tube (tip). Allow to dry.

3 Finally, pipe dots on the dominos and a dividing line down the centre of each one with dark brown icing in a bag with a no.2 tube (tip).

4 Leave to dry completely before stacking into piles for a game!

play time... Get a set of real dominos and copy the dot formations, remembering to pipe some dominos with the same number of spots on each side.

recipes chocolate cookies, royal icing
techniques piping with royal icing, flooding cookies with royal icing

velvet hearts

A lighter, individual way to enjoy red velvet cake – these little hearts will be adored by all.

you will need...

- ♡ 20cm (8in) square red velvet cake
- ♡ 6cm (2½in) heart-shaped cutter
- ♡ marshmallow fluff
- ♡ disposable piping (pastry) bag
- ♡ icing (confectioners') sugar to dust

1 Freeze the red velvet cake for 10 minutes to firm it slightly.

2 Using the heart-shaped cutter, gently cut out 25 heart shapes from the sponge cake. You should comfortably get five rows of five hearts. While still cold, slice each heart horizontally.

3 Fill the piping (pastry) bag with marshmallow fluff and snip a 1.5cm (½in) opening at the tip. Pipe a blob of the fluff onto the bottom half of each heart and gently sandwich together with the top half.

4 Dust with a little icing (confectioners') sugar and serve.

use it up...
A 20cm (8in) square cake will make 25 sandwiched hearts with some leftovers, which would be perfect for cake pops (see Making cake pops in Techniques).

recipes red velvet cake, marshmallow fluff
techniques piping buttercream

wedded bliss

These individual wedding cakes will delight guests. Experiment with flavours and colour schemes, and remember to warn the diners about the lollipop sticks inside!

you will need...

- ♡ 12 muffin-size vanilla cupcakes
- ♡ 12 standard vanilla cupcakes
- ♡ 200g (7oz) apricot glaze, warmed
- ♡ sugarpaste: 1.2kg (2lb 10oz) white
- ♡ 144 white fondant spiral roses dusted with white lustre dust
- ♡ 12 lollipop sticks
- ♡ 60ml (4 tbsp) white soft-peak royal icing
- ♡ piping (pastry) bag with no.2 tube (tip)
- ♡ ribbon to trim

1 Smear warmed apricot glaze on the outside of all the cupcakes.

2 Roll out a large plum-sized ball of sugarpaste to a 12cm (4¾in) circle. Cover a muffin-sized cupcake and rub the edges smooth. Repeat for the other muffin-sized cupcakes.

3 Roll out a small plum-sized ball of sugarpaste to a 10cm (4in) circle. Cover a standard cupcake and rub the edges smooth. Repeat for the other standard cupcakes.

4 Check the height of the stacked tiers allowing a 2.5cm (1in) gap between. Trim each lollipop stick to reach halfway through the depth of the top cake (you do not want it poking through the top!). Push the

stick vertically into the centre of the base cupcake, then position the smaller cupcake on top.

5 Use white royal icing in a piping (pastry) bag with a no.2 tube (tip) to fix 12 spiral roses between the two layers, flush with the edge of the bottom tier. Work round, positioning them at quarter turns and then fill in the gaps like numbers on a clock.

6 Trim with ribbon around the bases, securing with a dot of royal icing.

tiers of joy...
If your cupcakes have flat tops, use a ball of sugarpaste to help separate the tiers. Domed cupcakes should not require this.

recipes vanilla sponge cake, royal icing
techniques covering cakes with sugarpaste, making fondant flowers

teatime classic

An individual mini Victoria sponge, topped with a simple sugar rose, is surely everyone's idea of the perfect afternoon tea!

you will need...

- ♡ 36 standard vanilla cupcakes baked in simple paper cases
- ♡ 45ml (3 tbsp) light green soft-peak royal icing
- ♡ disposable piping (pastry) bag
- ♡ sugarpaste: 75g (2½oz) pink
- ♡ 200g (7oz) raspberry jam
- ♡ icing (confectioners') sugar for dusting
- ♡ paper doily

1 Fill the piping (pastry) bag with light green royal icing and snip the tip into a 3mm (⅛in) 'V'-shape.

2 On a large sheet of baking parchment, pipe three 2cm (¾in) leaves each pointing outwards from the centre in a triangular shape. Repeat to make 18 leaf formations.

3 Roll 18 spiral roses from the pink sugarpaste. Affix one to the centre of each leaf formation with a dab of green icing. Leave to dry.

4 Remove the paper cases from the cupcakes and smooth any rough edges on the cakes.

5 Sandwich the cupcake bases together in pairs using raspberry jam.

6 Using a paper doily as a stencil, lightly dust the tops of the cakes with icing (confectioners') sugar.

7 With a dab of light green icing, affix the flowers and leaves on top of each sandwich and serve.

fruity flavours ...

Make a lavender and blackcurrant variation using lavender sugar instead of caster (superfine) sugar in the basic recipe, omitting the vanilla extract, and using blackcurrant jam and purple roses.

recipes vanilla sponge cake, royal icing

techniques piping with royal icing, making fondant flowers, piping leaves

fabulous favours

These mini wedding cakes on a stick make memorable wedding favours or a kooky treat for a bridal shower. Go for girly pink or opt for classic white!

you will need...

- ♡ ingredients as for cake pops (see Making cake pops)
- ♡ 30–45ml (2–3 tbsp) each pale pink and bright pink soft-peak royal icing
- ♡ 2 piping (pastry) bags with no.2 tubes (tips)
- ♡ 20 pink fondant spiral roses
- ♡ 2cm (¾in) and 3cm (1in) round cutters
- ♡ cocktail sticks (toothpicks)

1 Prepare the cake ball mix. Instead of rolling balls, gently compress the moist crumbs into 2cm (¾in) and 3cm (1in) round cutters and push out 20 cork shapes in each size. Place on baking parchment and chill in the freezer for 10 minutes.

2 Prepare the Candy Melts as per the Technique instructions. Dip 3cm (1in) of the end of a lollipop stick into the mixture and insert it into the bottom of one of the larger cork shapes.

3 Level the tops of the smaller cakes and pierce in the centre halfway down into the cake with a cocktail stick (toothpick). Place all pieces on baking parchment and return to the freezer for 10 minutes.

4 Remove from the freezer and swirl the bases in the Candy Melts mixture. Push the sticks into the oasis or polystyrene to dry. Then swirl the top pieces on the cocktail sticks (toothpicks) and affix to the bases while still wet. Leave to set then carefully twist out the cocktail sticks (toothpicks) from the tops.

5 Pipe loops and a straight line of pale pink royal icing around the edge of the bottom tier and the top of the top tier. Pipe alternate bright and pale pink dots around the join.

6 Use pale pink royal icing to affix a spiral rose to the top of each cake pop, covering the hole left by the cocktail stick (toothpick).

recipes vanilla sponge cake, royal icing
techniques piping with royal icing, making fondant flowers, making cake pops

perfumed perfection

These elegant mini French macarons are flavoured with crystallized roses and violets for a treat that smells as sublime as it tastes.

you will need...

- ♡ ingredients as for French macarons (see Recipes)
- ♡ 20g (¾oz) each crystallized rose and violet petals
- ♡ white chocolate ganache
- ♡ pink and lilac gel food colourings
- ♡ 2.5ml (½ tsp) each rose water and violet essence (or ground Parma Violet sweets)
- ♡ disposable piping (pastry) bag with 1cm (⅜in) opening

1 Separately grind 5g (⅛oz) each of crystallized rose and violet petals to a fine powder. Divide the sugar and almond mixes in step 2 of the macaron recipe into two batches and add the rose powder to one and the violet powder to the other.

2 Divide the egg whites in step 3 of the recipe into two batches and add pink food colouring to one and lilac to the other in the latter stage of whisking. Tip the almond mixtures on top of their respective coloured meringues in step 5 of the recipe.

3 Continue with the recipe to mix the batter then use the piping (pastry) bag to pipe the macaron shells.

4 Lightly crush the remaining crystallized rose and violet petals with a rolling pin; sprinkle a little on the respective wet macaron shells. Leave the trays of shells to dry out for 20 minutes until a skin forms then bake as per the recipe instructions.

5 Divide the white chocolate ganache into two batches and tint one light pink and the other lilac. Flavour the pink ganache with rose water essence and the lilac ganache with the violet essence (or finely ground Parma Violet sweets).

6 Sandwich the cooled macaron shells together with their respective coloured ganaches. Before it sets, roll the macarons in the remaining crushed crystallized petals.

recipes french macarons, white chocolate ganache
techniques piping macarons

banana bows

Whoopie pies are not traditionally decorated, but they can be just as versatile as cupcakes. These chocolate-coated banana mini whoopies are embellished with a pretty fondant bow.

you will need...

- ♡ 48 banana mini whoopie shells
- ♡ marshmallow fluff
- ♡ 150g (5¼oz) milk chocolate ganache
- ♡ sugarpaste: 100g (3½oz) pale yellow
- ♡ comb modelling tool
- ♡ 30ml (2 tbsp) pale yellow soft-peak royal icing
- ♡ piping (pastry) bag with no.2 tube (tip)

1 Take the cooled whoopie shells and dip the tops of 24 of them in milk chocolate ganache.

2 Place on a wire rack and allow to set then sandwich one coated and one uncoated shell together with a generous blob of marshmallow fluff.

3 Roll out the pale yellow sugarpaste to an even 3mm (⅛in) thickness and model 24 miniature bows. Use the comb tool to make stitching marks on their edges. Set aside to firm up slightly.

4 Using the piping (pastry) bag, pipe a dot of pale yellow royal icing onto the top of each whoopie. Carefully lift and press a bow into place in the centre of each pie.

fun with filling...
You can use a spoon or palette knife to fill the whoopies with marshmallow fluff, or you could try piping it in with different shaped tubes (tips) for different decorative effects.

recipes banana mini whoopie pie shells, milk chocolate ganache, marshmallow fluff
techniques piping with buttercream, making fondant novelties

fruity pavlovas

A canapé version of the popular dessert – these mini meringue nests are beautiful to look at and melt-in-the-mouth good!

you will need...

- ♡ ingredients as for mini meringues (see Recipes)
- ♡ 100ml (3½fl oz) whipping cream
- ♡ 100g (3½oz) mango, diced into 0.5cm (⅛in) cubes
- ♡ 24 raspberries
- ♡ flesh and seeds of 1 passion fruit
- ♡ 100g (3½oz) redcurrants
- ♡ piping (pastry) bag with 1.5cm (½in) star tube (tip)

1 Fill the piping (pastry) bag with the meringue batter and pipe flat 5cm (2in) circles onto a baking sheet lined with baking parchment. Immediately pipe a border of more meringue around the edge of each circle to build a nest shape. Pipe a second layer of border if necessary. Use a teaspoon handle to wiggle a hollow if the nest collapses inwards.

2 Bake and cool the meringues as per the recipe instructions.

3 Using an electric mixer with a large bowl, whip the cream until it is thick and glossy.

4 Spoon a little whipped cream into the hollow of each pavlova nest.

5 Top each one with several tiny pieces of fruit; three cubes of mango, one raspberry, two or three redcurrants and a drizzle of passion fruit. Serve immediately.

follow the seasons... Try seasonal variations with different fruits such as blackberries, blueberries or blackcurrants.

recipes mini meringues

tea ceremony

Green tea powder is a widely used ingredient in Japanese desserts. In these Madeleines it is combined with sesame and chocolate to glorious effect.

you will need...

- ♡ ingredients as for Madeleines (see Recipes)
- ♡ 5ml (1 tsp) matcha (green tea) powder, sifted
- ♡ 75g (2¾oz) dark chocolate ganache
- ♡ 75g (2¾oz) white chocolate ganache
- ♡ 30ml (2 tbsp) each dark brown and ivory soft-peak royal icing
- ♡ 30g (1oz) white sesame seeds
- ♡ 2 disposable piping (pastry) bags with no.2 tubes (tips)

1 Follow the recipe for standard Madeleines, adding the sifted matcha powder with the flour. Mix and bake the cakes as per the recipe instructions.

2 Allow to cool completely. Meanwhile gently warm the dark and white chocolate ganaches in mugs in the microwave on reduced power.

3 Dip half of the Madeleines partly in the ganaches and immediately dip the edge of the wet ganache into the sesame seeds. Stand on a wire rack for the ganache to set.

4 For the remaining Madeleines, separately fill the piping (pastry) bags with dark brown and ivory royal icing and pipe lines in a fan arrangement following the scallop shape of the cakes on the top surface of each Madeleine. Allow to set.

orient express... Japanese stores sell matcha powder but it may be easier to find online. It's not cheap but a little lasts a long time. If you can't get matcha, fresh plain Madeleines are still heavenly.

recipes madeleines, royal icing, dark chocolate ganache
techniques piping with royal icing

pretty in pink

Several recipes go into making these cute mini éclairs but the piping and daisy decorations on them are simple and effective.

you will need...

- ♡ 24 mini choux fingers
- ♡ sugarpaste: 25g (¾oz) white
- ♡ miniature daisy plunger cutter
- ♡ crème patissière
- ♡ glacé icing (half the recipe quantity)
- ♡ 45ml (3 tbsp) white soft-peak royal icing
- ♡ pink and yellow gel or paste food colourings
- ♡ piping gun with syringe nozzle
- ♡ 3 disposable piping (pastry) bags, 1 with 5mm (³⁄₁₆in) opening, 1 with no.2 tube (tip), 1 with no.3 tube (tip)

1 Roll out the white sugarpaste and cut out 24 mini daisies with the plunger cutter. Set aside.

2 Using a touch of gel or paste food colouring, tint the crème patissière pink.

3 Meanwhile, in a medium-size bowl, tint the glacé icing pink too.

4 Fill up the piping gun with the cold crème patissière and inject it into the centre of each cooled choux finger.

5 Fill a piping (pastry) bag with glacé icing and cut a 5mm (³⁄₁₆in) opening in the tip. Pipe ovals of icing on top of each éclair, using a cocktail stick (toothpick) to encourage it to spread fairly

evenly in each direction. Allow to set for 10 minutes.

6 Fill a piping (pastry) bag with a no.3 tube (tip) with white soft-peak royal icing and pipe freehand zigzags across the pink glacé icing.

7 Carefully press a fondant daisy into the wet icing on the corner of each mini éclair.

8 Tint the remaining white icing yellow and use to fill a piping (pastry) bag with a no.2 tube (tip). Pipe yellow centres onto the fondant daisies and serve as soon as possible.

---

recipes choux pastry, royal icing, glacé icing, crème patissière

techniques piping with royal icing, piping choux buns and fingers, making fondant flowers

citrus bites

These lightest of tarts are barely more than a mouthful; the sweet pastry and sharp lemon combination will have you reaching for another… and another…

you will need...

- ♡ sweet pastry, chilled and ready to roll
- ♡ flour to roll out pastry
- ♡ 7–8cm (2¾–3in) round cutter
- ♡ lemon curd filling
- ♡ zest of 1 lemon, cut into very fine strips
- ♡ 15g (1 tbsp) granulated (table) sugar
- ♡ 75ml (2½fl oz) water
- ♡ icing (confectioners') sugar for dusting

1 Preheat the oven to 200°C/400°F/ Gas 6 and lightly grease a 12-hole mini muffin tin (pan).

2 Using a little flour, roll the pastry out to an even 5mm (³⁄₁₆in) thickness and cut out 20 circles of pastry with the round cutter. Use your fingers to gently press them a little thinner and wider then place the pastry circles into the wells of the muffin tin (pan).

2 Prick the surface of each case with a fork then cover each one with a square of baking parchment and a few baking beans.

3 Bake for 10–12 minutes then remove the paper and beans.

4 Fill the cases three-quarters full with lemon curd filling.

5 Bake for a further 10 minutes. Allow to cool slightly in the tin (pan) before transferring to a wire rack.

6 Meanwhile, boil the lemon zest strips in the water and granulated (table) sugar for a few minutes until they crystallize. Pick out of the hot syrup with tongs and shape the strips into curls before they set.

7 When the tarts are cool, decorate with the zest curls and a dusting of icing (confectioners') sugar.

perfectly formed…
Use a small ball of pastry dough wrapped in cling film (plastic wrap) to push the pastry gently into the shape of the tin (pan).

recipes sweet pastry, lemon curd filling

café crème

These sophisticated individual profiteroles are filled with coffee crème patissière with a topping to match.

you will need...

- ♡ 24 mini choux buns
- ♡ crème patissière
- ♡ 10ml (2 tsp) good-quality instant espresso powder
- ♡ glacé icing (half the recipe quantity)
- ♡ 5ml (1 tsp) cocoa powder (unsweetened cocoa), sifted
- ♡ 45ml (3 tbsp) dark chocolate ganache
- ♡ 24 whole coffee beans
- ♡ piping gun with syringe nozzle
- ♡ 2 disposable piping (pastry) bags

1 During the final simmering stage of making the crème patissière, add 5ml (1 tsp) of the espresso powder. Allow to cool completely.
2 Meanwhile, in a medium-size bowl, mix the remaining espresso and cocoa powders into the glacé icing. It should coat the back of a spoon without dripping but not be so thick that it won't move at all.
3 When the crème patissière is cold, fill up the piping gun and inject it into the centre of each cooled choux bun.
4 Fill a piping (pastry) bag with the glacé icing and snip a 5mm (³⁄₁₆in) opening at the tip. Pipe 3cm (1in) filled circles of icing

on top of each choux bun and use a cocktail stick (toothpick) to encourage the icing to spread out evenly in each direction.
5 Fill a piping (pastry) bag with dark chocolate ganache and snip the tip into a 3mm (⅛in) 'V'-shaped point. Warm the bag in your hands for a minute so the ganache will pipe freely.
6 Squeeze the bag to make a trefoil of dark chocolate leaf shapes on top of each choux bun. Dot the centre with a whole coffee bean.

recipes choux pastry, glacé icing, dark chocolate ganache, crème patissière
techniques piping choux buns and fingers, piping leaves

templates

To download full-size printable PDFs of these templates go to:
www.bakeme.com/page/templates

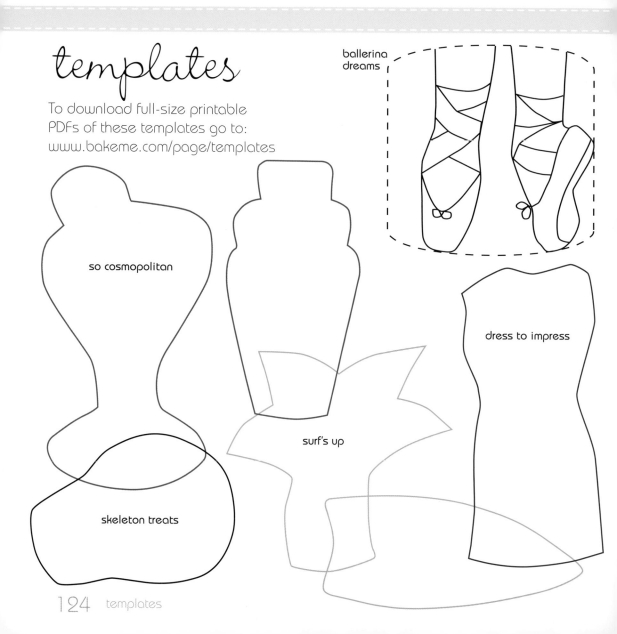

ballerina dreams

so cosmopolitan

dress to impress

surf's up

skeleton treats

suppliers

UK

Cakes Cookies & Crafts Shop
+44 (0)1732 463 573
www.cakescookiesandcrafts
shop.co.uk
General sugarcraft

CSN Stores
0800 917 5124
www.csnstores.co.uk
Wide range of miniature
silicone moulds

Divertimenti
0870 129 5026
www.divertimenti.co.uk
Mini Madeleine tin (pan)

Ikea
www.ikea.com
Inexpensive sets of small
sealable tubs for icing

Jane Asher
+44 (0)20 7584 6177
www.janeasher.com
Crystallized rose and violet petals
Sugarflair paste food colouring

Lakeland
+44 (0)1539 488100
www.lakeland.co.uk
Disposable piping (pastry)
bags, plain cupcake cases

Let's Cook @ Amazon
www.amazon.co.uk
Mini whoopie pie tin (pan)

Sainsburys
Stores nationwide
Silverspoon Mich Turner lustre
liquid, Dr Oetker sugarpaste
and coloured sugars

Squires
+44 (0)1252 260260
www.squires-shop.com
General sugarcraft with
excellent-quality cupcake cases

Steenbergs
+44 (0)1765 640088
www.steenbergs.co.uk
Matcha powder and fair
trade vanilla extract

USA

Global Sugar Art
+1 518 561 3039
www.globalsugarart.com
General sugarcraft

AUSTRALIA

Iced Affair
+61 (0)2 9519 3679
www.icedaffair.com.au
General sugarcraft

about the author

Sarah Trivuncic is a self-taught baker who has been writing one of the UK's best-known baking blogs, Maison Cupcake, since 2009. She began publishing cupcake pictures while practising for a street party and inspired by her love of American baking sites and French patisserie, has carried on writing about baking and family life at Maisoncupcake.com ever since.

When Sarah is not in the kitchen she can be found on Twitter or Facebook sharing news about the latest baking books, products and cake shops as well as her own recipes. Sarah was named 'best for good advice' among Channel 4 Food's 'Best Baking Blogs' in 2011 and was number one in the annual Cision UK Top 10 Baking and Confectionery blogs.

Sarah lives in London with her husband and young son. This is her first book.

acknowledgments

Many thanks to James, Grace, Sarah, Ame and all the team at David & Charles. Also to Jenny Fox-Proverbs for convincing me I could do this, to Sian Irvine for her magical photography and Helen Best-Shaw for keeping me sane and making me laugh. Thank you also to Jo, Ren, Naomi, Becky, Alis, Sarah, Jeanne and Nic for their help testing recipes.

I couldn't have written this without the support of my family and friends, both near and far, nor without the encouragement of the wonderful network of friends I've made since beginning to write my blog. I owe everyone a lot of cake and attention!

index

A DAVID & CHARLES BOOK
© F&W Media International, Ltd 2012

David & Charles is an imprint of F&W
Media International, Ltd
Brunel House, Forde Close, Newton
Abbot, TQ12 4PU, UK

F&W Media International, Ltd is a
subsidiary of F+W Media, Inc
10151 Carver Road, Cincinnati OH45242, USA

Text and Designs © Sarah Trivuncic 2012
Layout and Photography © F&W
Media International, Ltd 2012

First published in the UK and USA in 2012
Digital edition published in 2012

Layout of digital editions may vary depending
on reader hardware and display settings.

Names of manufacturers and product ranges are
provided for the information of readers, with no
intention to infringe copyright or trademarks.

A catalogue record for this book is
available from the British Library.

ISBN-13: 978-1-4463-0183-8 hardback
ISBN-10: 1-4463-0183-4 hardback

ISBN-13: 978-1-4463-5565-7 e-pub
ISBN-10: 1-4463-5565-9 e-pub

ISBN-13: 978-1-4463-5564-0 PDF
ISBN-10: 1-4463-5564-0 PDF

Hardback edition printed in China by RR Donnelley for:
F&W Media International, Ltd
Brunel House, Forde Close, Newton
Abbot, TQ12 4PU, UK

10 9 8 7 6 5 4 3 2 1

Acquisitions Editor: James Brooks
Assistant Editor: Grace Harvey
Project Editor: Ame Verso
Art Editor: Sarah Underhill
Designer Manager: Sarah Clark
Photographer: Sian Irvine
Production Controller: Kelly Smith

F+W Media publishes high quality books
on a wide range of subjects.
For more great book ideas visit: www.rucraft.co.uk

loved this book?

We've got all sorts of goodies up our sugary sleeves, so if you loved this book, visit our website to find out more!

www.bakeme.com

The Busy Girl's Guide to Cake Decorating

Ruth Clemens
ISBN-13: 978-1-4463-0164-7

Whether you're a time-starved baking expert or a cake decorating novice, this practical book shows you how to fit cake making at home into your busy lifestyle. These 25 gorgeous projects are ordered by how long they take to make, from as little as an hour!

Bake Me I'm Yours... Cupcake Celebration

Lindy Smith
ISBN-13: 978-0-7153-3770-7

Celebrate in style, with over 25 irresistible cupcake ideas from renowned sugarcrafter Lindy Smith. Add that special touch to every occasion with these amazing designs and tempting recipes, including sticky ginger, chocolate cherry and lemon polenta.

The Contemporary Cake Decorating Bible

Lindy Smith
ISBN-13: 978-0-7153-3836-0

Discover everything you need to know to create celebration cakes that are beautiful, unique and truly contemporary. Features over 150 techniques and more than 80 projects, including tiered cakes, wonky cakes, mini cakes, cupcakes and cookies.

Bake Me I'm Yours... Cake Pops

Carolyn White
ISBN-13: 978-1-4463-0137-1

A delicious collection of fun cake pop treats for every occasion, with over 40 colourful projects, from cute animals and romantic wedding rings, to creepy Halloween creatures and festive Christmas characters!

All details correct at time of printing.